I0693409

The Pleasure of Rum.

By Edo Cruz

Table of Contents.

Prologue: A Toast to Responsibility (and Good Humor)

Dear reader thirsty for knowledge (and possibly something stronger),

Welcome to "The Pleasure of Rum," a spirited journey through the history, culture, and traditions of Cuban rum.

If you've opened this book, it's because you share two passions with me: Cuba and the noble art of enjoying a good drink. Or maybe you were just looking for a mojito recipe and ended up in the wrong aisle. In any case, prepare yourself for a journey as intense as aged Havana Club and as refreshing as a piña colada in Varadero.

But before you start salivating thinking about daiquiris and Cuba libres, let me put on the hat of responsibility for a moment (yes, that horrible hat nobody wants to wear at parties).

IMPORTANT WARNING (read in a grave voice with dramatic background music):

Excessive alcohol consumption is harmful to health. This book is intended solely for adults of legal drinking age. If you're underage, close this book immediately and go read something more appropriate, like "The Adventures of Pepito the Teetotaler" or "Fruit Juices: The Path to Sober Fun."

Rum, like all alcoholic beverages, can be treacherous. It's like that friend who encourages you to do crazy things: fun in the moment, but leaves you with a moral (and physical) hangover the next day.

So remember: drink in moderation, never drive after drinking, and for Hemingway's sake, don't try to impress anyone by drinking more than you can handle. Nobody wants to be "that guy" at the party, you know, the one who ends up declaring eternal love to a palm tree thinking it's Shakira.

That said, let's get back to the fun stuff.

This book is a tribute to that golden beverage that has witnessed (and probably caused) countless historical moments, memorable parties, and questionable decisions. Cuban rum isn't just a drink it's a character in the great novel of Cuban history, as important as Martí, as omnipresent as the Malecón, and definitely more fun than an 8 AM history class.

In the pages that follow, we'll explore:

1. The History of Cuban Rum: From its humble origins as "rat poison" for slaves to its current status as the elixir of Caribbean gods. Spoiler alert: it involves pirates, revolutionaries, and probably some epic headaches.

2. The Art of Distillation: Or how Cubans turned sugarcane into the nectar of the gods. We warn you that this chapter may contain more chemistry than your high school memories, but we promise to make it more entertaining.

3. Iconic Cocktails: Because, let's be honest, nobody drinks straight rum unless they're desperate or they're Ernest Hemingway.

You'll learn to prepare the perfect mojito, the daiquiri that would make Floridita cry, and the Cuba libre that will make you feel freer than a seagull on the Malecón (until the next morning, at least).

4. Rum in Cuban Culture: From Santería to salsa, rum has left its golden mark on every aspect of Cuban life. Discover how a simple drink became an integral part of a nation's identity.

5. Legends and Anecdotes: Because there's nothing like a good story to accompany a good drink. Prepare to laugh, be surprised, and possibly question the veracity of official history.

This book is for rum lovers, the curious about Cuban culture, and for those who enjoy a good story with a touch of humor. It's not for teetotalers, minors, or those who think rum is "just another drink." If you're in this last category, we suggest you close this book and go have some tea.

So, dear adult and responsible reader, prepare yourself for a journey that will stimulate your senses, expand your knowledge, and possibly give you some ideas for your next party (or to impress your friends at the bar with curious facts about rum).

Remember: this book is best enjoyed with good rum by your side, but if you decide to follow this advice, do so in moderation. We are not responsible for embarrassing phone calls to ex-partners, questionable taste tattoos, or impromptu Celia Cruz karaoke sessions at 3 in the morning.

And now, without further ado, let's raise our imaginary (or real, we don't judge) glasses and toast to Cuban rum, to Cuba, and to you, brave reader, who are about to embark on this alcoholic and literary adventure.

Cheers, and may rum be with you! (But not too much, eh?)

Chapter I: Cuban Rum: A History That Will Leave You Dizzy (with Laughter)

Set sail with me on a journey through the tempestuous sea of rum! From pirates to virgin islands, this tropical beverage has more stories than a parrot on a ship. Every sip is an adventure in itself! Knowledge, anecdotes, and mysteries blend in this ocean of flavor. Raise your glass and toast to the treasures that await us! May high tide carry us toward new adventures and joyful drinking sprees!

Ah, the wise and alcoholic Oscar Wilde! With his words, he reminds us that rum is like a magic mirror: at first, everything is joy and fantasy, but then it confronts you with harsh reality. So, drink in moderation and keep your sanity! Because after the third glass, who knows what reality we'll discover! □□ (Oscar Wilde).

"You don't notice it, but the rum runs out" (Jack Sparrow). (And when it runs out, that's when you really notice it, right, Jack?)

"But why is the rum gone? Is this a dream? If it were one, there would be rum" (Jack Sparrow). (Calm down, Jack, maybe you just need to check under your hat)

"Fifteen men on the dead man's chest. Yo, ho, ho and a bottle of rum" (Robert Louis Stevenson). (Just one bottle for fifteen men? Now that's a pirate tragedy)

"I wanted to drown my sorrows in alcohol, but the damn things learned to swim" (Frida Kahlo). (Maybe you should have taught them to dive, Frida)

"Alcohol may be man's worst enemy. And doesn't the Bible say to love your enemies?" (Frank Sinatra). (Frank, always so biblical and so thirsty)

"Alcohol is the anesthesia that helps us endure the operation of living" (George Bernard Shaw).

(Operation? I'd say it's more like a three-ring circus)

"I may be drunk, miss, but in the morning I'll be sober and you'll still be ugly" (Winston Churchill). (Churchill, the master of diplomacy... when he's sober)

"The true character of men appears when they're drunk" (Charlie Chaplin). (And sometimes, so does the contents of their stomach)

"Alcohol gives you infinite patience to tolerate stupidity" (Sammy Davis Jr.). (Or maybe it just makes you seem more stupid than the rest)

I truly believe that all Cubans at some point in their lives have tried rum or at least some of its mixtures or versions. What's certain is that if a cat has seven lives, Cuban rum has more than a thousand.

I think if we measured the amount of liters of this elixir consumed daily in Cuba, many would be surprised and others would start reflecting. (And some couldn't even count to a thousand after so much rum)

This is how on this unique island, from a very young age I've smelled around me, directly or indirectly, the different aromas of such a popular beverage and I've noticed glasses of all sizes, models, and states of use employed for such a popular pastime. (From fine crystal glasses to coconuts cut in half, rum doesn't discriminate!)

A drink of good Cuban rum will always be one of the best ways for celebration to become a party of spirit and body, because drinking rum—if not overdone—grants cultural status when making a toast. Even more than beer, which tends toward noise and expansion. (Because nothing says "I'm culturally sophisticated" like drinking rum at 11 in the morning)

The truth is that the history of Cuban rum is as old as colonization itself, and with various versions, hahaha.

Rum is a byproduct of the juice extracted from sugarcane that Admiral Christopher Columbus brought to the Island on his second voyage to this continent. (Apparently, Columbus thought: "Since I'm here, why not bring something to make the party more fun?")

What follows is known: the roots of the cane from the Canary Islands took hold in the virgin and fertile Cuban soil where it found an ideal microclimate to grow, mainly around indigenous villages and granted estates. (Sugarcane: the plant that said "I like this place, I'm staying")

Initially it was the indigenous people (the indigenous, always the indigenous a smile) who discovered its virtues by squeezing the stems to drink the sweet juice.

Later, the sugar mill, refineries, and sugar plantations worked by African slaves took charge of multiplying production. (Because nothing says "progress" like exploiting others to make alcohol, right?)

By the end of the 16th century, Cuba was considered the world's sugar reserve so that later rum would become a world-renowned liquor, obtained as a byproduct of such sweet nectar, presiding over celebrations, romantic encounters, and happy moments... (And also presiding over many bad decisions and epic hangovers)

Another version tells that since 1650 in this Caribbean area there already existed a rum manufactured by pirates and corsairs who prowled the zone, called "rumbullion." (Because even pirates needed something to make their ship parties more interesting)

In Cuba, on the other hand, it's told that with the extermination of its first inhabitants, around the 16th century.

With the arrival of black slaves torn from their lands, the story continued. (Nothing like a little genocide and slavery to liven up the party, eh?)

It's said that slaves were accustomed to drinking what they called "guarapo," obtained from the fermentation of yuca and corn. Then, they moved on to extracting juice from sugarcane which became a competent and quality beverage.

(Because if they're going to exploit you, at least let it be with a good drink in hand)

Now, go and enjoy a good Cuban rum, but remember: drink responsibly. After all, we don't want you to end up like Jack Sparrow, looking for rum on a desert island and talking to palm trees. Cheers!

The Evolution: From Indigenous Discovery to Global Industry

3. The First Drinks: The indigenous discovered its virtues by squeezing the stems.

4. Evolution: From sugar mill to refinery, from plantation to global industry.

Alternative Versions

- Pirates and their "rumbullion" since 1650.

- Slaves and their "guarapo" of yuca and corn, then from cane.

Conclusion: An Elixir with History.

Cuban rum, from its humble origins to becoming a quality beverage in the 19th century, is more than a liquor. It's history, culture, and tradition in every sip.

As Oscar Wilde would say (if he had tried Cuban rum): "Rum is like a magic mirror: at first, everything is joy and fantasy, but then it confronts you with harsh reality. Drink in moderation and keep your sanity!"

And that's how various brands with distilleries that were built in Cárdenas, Santiago de Cuba, Cienfuegos, and Havana emerged in the country. (Because, apparently, one city couldn't contain so much... alcoholic spirit)

At the same time, several brands established themselves in the world, among them Matusalén, Jiquí, Bocoy, Campeón, Obispo, San Carlos, Albuerne, Castillo, Bacardí. (A more impressive lineup than the Avengers of the rum world)

But the best known of all since the Cuban rum industry was reorganized and expanded has been the old "Havana Club" brand founded in Cárdenas originally in 1878—dedicated to export, and whose emblem is La Giraldilla, a small statue that symbolizes the city of Havana. (Because nothing says "drink rum" like a little statue atop a castle)

Since 1993 this brand is presented under the Franco-Cuban firm Havana Club International S.A.—the French company Pernod-Ricard handles its worldwide distribution—and produces the Aged White, Three Years Special, Seven Years Reserve and Fifteen Years, in addition to the younger Cuban Barrel Proof and the Extra Aged Maximum, all of great national and international acceptance.

(Because the French know about wines, but apparently they also know how to move rum around the world)

For a good time Havana Club was alone in the world market.

Currently, other Cuban brands, no less important, have managed to strengthen themselves in the world, among them: Mulata, Arecha, Legendario, Varadero, Santiago, Santero, and Caney. (So many options that one no longer knows if they're in a liquor store or at a Cuban superhero convention)

Ave, Caesar, Morituri te salutant (Or as we say in Cuba: "Cheers, we're going to get really happy!")

Let's make something clear, my rum-loving friends, I know perfectly well that drinking excessively is a risk, like almost any excess in this life. Under no type of excuse would I encourage anyone to drink without savoring, that is, without taking the time and pleasure to enjoy it. (Because drinking rum is an art, not a race)

That said, I appreciate nothing in life like a good drink of rum, needless to say it's an unprecedented pleasure to find your favorite poison and drink it sweetly, without hurry. That class one has when drinking rum is a sign of good taste, playing with it in your throat, the thick tears on the edges of your glass, being able to appreciate how it slides inside you and how sometimes it causes that effect that makes you curse like any good pirate, all of this is really a great pleasure. (Who needs poetry when you have a bottle of rum?)

Chapter II: Cuban Rum and Its Distant Cousins: A Tour Through Cuba's Clandestine Bar.

Cuba is famous for its alcoholic beverages, but Cuban rum without its urban versions wouldn't be street culture in our country. Everyone who enjoys "lifting their elbow" around the world has probably tasted the Island through Havana Club, Mulata, or Santiago rum. And the same happens with cocktails: the Daiquiri, Cuba Libre, and Mojito are probably in all the bars of the world. (Because nothing says "international diplomacy" like sharing a hangover)

But in Cuba there are many other drinks that foreigners and even some Cubans don't know about, true alcoholic inventions that saw the light during the Special Period as alternatives to the very scarce production of the Cuban rum industry in the 90s. They are drinks only suitable for "professionals," for people who have throats and hearts of titanium, people who live their lives at the limit of extreme sports (a smile). (Because when life gives you lemons... well, in Cuba apparently you make rum)

I want to share some curiosities, recipes, and names of these creations only with the intention of laughing at that reality of the past, and not to provide chemical formulas harmful to health. (Warning: The author is not responsible for any temporary blindness, loss of dignity, or embarrassing dancing that may result from these recipes)

So there you have it, friends. The history of Cuban rum: a mixture of ingenuity, resistance, and probably a bit of madness. Because when life gives you sugarcane, you make rum. And when life doesn't give you even that, you invent something even stronger! Cheers, and remember: drink responsibly, or at least with a friend who can record your antics for posterity. Until the next drink!

Let's start, buddy...

The "train spark": The Express Train to Dizziness Land

Also known as "azuquín," "tiger's tooth," "jump backwards," "man and earth," etc. The Train Spark is one of the strongest and most famous homemade drinks in Cuba. The name is quite graphic, but in case you don't get it, imagine a train at full speed braking suddenly. The sparks that fly are the neurons in your brain screaming "Help!"

Warning: If you ever dare to try it, make sure you have good medical insurance and perhaps an updated will. It's a real knockout for inexperienced drinkers. Even Mike Tyson would think twice before facing this liquid heavyweight!

The "planchao": The Tetra Pack from Hell

The planchao is like the younger brother of the Train Spark. It's the gourmet option for those who don't want (or can't) afford a bigger bottle. It's the perfect appetizer for those who think: "Why do I need a liver anyway?"

The best (or worst) part is the ritual of sharing it. Nothing says "true friendship" like passing a cardboard box full of alcohol from mouth to mouth. Who needs glasses when you have friends willing to share their germs with you? It's like a blood pact, but with more chances of ending up in the emergency room.

"90-Proof Alcohol": Because 89 Degrees Weren't Enough

Thanks to Louis Joseph Gay-Lussac, we know that sake has 20 degrees, tequila 55, and vodka 40. But in Cuba they said: "What if we take it to the extreme?" Thus was born 90-Proof Alcohol, a drink that makes vodka look like tap water.

It's so strong that Cubans use it to:

1. Disinfect wounds
2. Clean engines

3. Remove tiles

4. And, occasionally, drink it (if you have a burning desire to visit the hospital)

The "Guarapin": When Desperation Meets Home Chemistry

Ingredients:

- 3/4 bodega alcohol (yes, the one you use for cleaning)

- 1/4 sugarcane juice (to give it that "healthy" touch)

- A pinch of madness

Instructions:

1. Mix the ingredients

2. Wait 10 minutes (or until you see double)

3. Remove the grease that forms on top (or don't, if you want an extra "nutritious" experience)

4. Drink and pray!

Other Names that Would Make a Professional Bartender Cry:

- Mafuco

- Troublemaker

- Rat Killer

- The Illegal

- Brake Fluid

- Wait for Me on the Ground

- Climb Up the Pole

- Go to Sleep My Child

Remember, these drinks were born in desperate times, when finding a decent bottle of rum was as difficult as finding a unicorn in Havana.

Some still exist because, as the saying goes, "what's bad doesn't pass, it always stays." Or maybe because after trying them, nobody remembers how to return to normalcy.

Conclusion: A Toast to Creativity (and Liver Survival)

These creations are a testament to Cuban ingenuity and human determination to find ways to... relax? forget? defy death? Whatever the reason, let's remember these drinks with a mixture of amazement, horror, and respect. And please, if you ever visit Cuba, stick to the classics. Your liver, your dignity, and your future grandchildren will thank you.

Cheers! (And may God have mercy on our souls and our livers)

Chapter III: Son 14: The Legend of the Drink That Made You Dance... on the Floor.

Dear readers thirsty for knowledge (and possibly something stronger), prepare yourselves for a journey through time as dizzying as a night of drinking in Havana. We're going back to the 80s, an era when Cuban ingenuity reached new heights (or depths, depending on how you look at it) in the world of alcoholic beverages.

We're talking about Cárdenas, a city that not only gave the world the famous Havana Club rum, but was also the setting for the birth of a mythical creature that made the bravest drinkers tremble: "Son 14," also affectionately known as "Wait for Me on the Ground." Yes, friends, a name that is a complete statement of intentions.

The Birth of a Legend.

Imagine the scene: it's just another day in Cárdenas, the sun shines with the typical intensity of the Caribbean, and suddenly, as if fallen from heaven (or more likely, from the back of a truck of dubious origin), a drink in small soda bottles arrives in the city. Its innocent appearance and sweet taste fooled everyone. "A refreshing soft drink!" exclaimed the local experts, the same ones who could distinguish between 50 types of rum blindfolded, but who had apparently lost their common sense along with some neurons along the way.

The first to try it were, as could not be otherwise, the young adventurers always in search of new experiences. "It tastes like glory!" said some. "It's like drinking a rainbow," others affirmed, although they were probably already seeing rainbows by that point. Little did they know they were about to become guinea pigs in one of the most infamous alcoholic experiments in Cuban history.

The Mystery of the Name.

Now then, why "Son 14"? Ah, here's where legend mixes with reality, like a good Cuba libre, but much more dangerous. Some theories:

1. The Musical Theory: Some say it was named in honor of the popular Cuban son band "Son 14." Imagine the scene: the creators of this drink, sitting in a bar, listening to "Son 14" and thinking: "You know what would make this music even better? A drink that makes you see 14 of everything!"

2. The Mathematical Theory: Others claim that after 14 sips, you saw 14 pink elephants dancing salsa. Although, let's be honest, if you made it to 14 sips, you probably weren't counting anything anymore.

3. The Knockout Theory: The darkest of all suggests that 14 was the average number of seconds it took you to hit the floor after drinking. Cuban efficiency at its finest.

Whatever the truth, the name "Son 14" quickly became synonymous with a night you probably wouldn't remember, but your body (and your dignity) would never forget.

The Devil's Composition.

Now, prepare yourselves for the technical part, the one that would make any respectable mixologist cry and possibly provoke a riot in any bartending school. Son 14, this platypus of bars, this liquid monstrosity, was one part alcohol to nine parts syrup. Yes, you read that right: ONE part alcohol and NINE parts syrup.

It was as if someone had looked at the traditional cocktail recipe and said: "You know what?

Let's do it backwards and see what happens." And what happened was that they created a drink that was basically a liquid dessert with the ability to knock out an elephant.

Legend has it that the alcohol used was of such proof that it could have been used as rocket fuel. The syrup, on the other hand, was so sweet it probably contributed to the increase in diabetes cases in the region. Together, they formed a combination as lethal as it was delicious, a real "sweet punch" that made you fall with a smile on your face.

Side Effects (or Primary, depending on how you look at it).

Now, my friends, we come to the part everyone was waiting for: the infamous effects of Son 14. Prepare yourselves for a list that would make even the bravest of drinkers think twice:

1. Instant Collapse: Faster than saying "Cheers!" It was as if your legs suddenly decided they no longer wanted to be part of your body. One moment you were standing, boasting about your alcohol resistance, and the next you were one with the floor. Gravity 1 - Dignity 0.

2. Guaranteed Ridicule: Son 14 was perfect for those who always wanted to be the life of the party, but for the wrong reasons. It gave you superhuman confidence to do things like declare your eternal love to a palm tree, attempt a breakdancing routine (without knowing how to dance), or try to convince everyone you could talk to fish. Spoiler alert: you couldn't.

3. Selective Amnesia: Because what happens after Son 14, stays with Son 14. It was as if your brain said: "You know what, better not save any of this." A natural defense mechanism, probably.

4. Epic Hangover: If you thought your previous hangovers were bad, Son 14 taught you what a real hangover was.

It was as if a truck had run you over, and then backed up to make sure. The good news: you generally didn't remember how you'd gotten to that state.

5. Superhero Abilities (temporary): For some reason, Son 14 made you believe you had superpowers. People trying to fly, thinking they could read minds, or believing they were invisible. Spoiler alert again: they weren't, to everyone's embarrassment.

The Birthday Anecdote.

No legend would be complete without its collection of anecdotes, and Son 14 has its share in abundance. But there's one that stands out above the rest, a story that has been passed down from generation to generation, whispered in bar corners and told with a mixture of horror and fascination.

It's rumored that once, due to a monumental error (or perhaps a very bad joke), they served Son 14 at a children's birthday party. Yes, you read that right. A children's birthday party. Imagine the scene: balloons, clowns, a piñata, and bottles of what everyone thought was an innocent soft drink.

The result was, as you can imagine, chaotic at best and apocalyptic at worst.

What began as a typical children's party quickly turned into something out of a surrealist film. Ten-year-olds discussing international politics, mothers doing handstands in the middle of the living room, and grandmothers who suddenly remembered that in their youth they had been limbo champions.

The climax came when 85-year-old Grandma Conchita, known until then for her fondness for soap operas and her cat collection, climbed on the table and started leading a conga line that lasted, according to witnesses, three hours and went around the block seven times.

The party ended with the arrival of the firefighters (apparently, someone decided it was a good time to roast a pig in the living room), three clowns having existential crises, and a group of children who swore they would never drink soda again in their lives.

The parent-teacher meeting that followed this incident is the stuff of legends. It's said that the school principal, after hearing the reports, simply took off her glasses, sighed deeply, and said: "I think we all need a drink after this." Although, curiously, nobody suggested Son 14.

The Legacy.

Like all legends, Son 14 had a life as short as it was intense.

It appeared out of nowhere, like an alcoholic comet, illuminated (or rather clouded) the minds of Cárdenas residents for a brief but unforgettable period, and then disappeared without a trace, like a drunken ninja in the night.

Its disappearance was as mysterious as its appearance. Some say the government intervened, fearing that Son 14 could be used as a chemical weapon. Others claim that the creators themselves, terrified by what they had unleashed, destroyed all existing stock and retired to a monastery in the mountains. The most plausible theory, however, is that they simply ran out of syrup.

What's certain is that nobody really missed it, except perhaps the ice manufacturers, who saw their sales drop drastically. After all, who needs ice when your drink leaves you cold in a matter of seconds?

Conclusion: A Toast to Son 14.

Although it's no longer with us, Son 14 lives on in the memory of those who tried it and survived to tell about it. It's a reminder that sometimes Cuban creativity can be as dangerous as it is delicious, and that not everything that comes in a pretty bottle is good for you.

Son 14 went down in history as the drink that could make even those with two left feet dance, although that dancing usually happened on the floor. It was the terror of livers, the best friend of those who wanted to forget, and possibly the reason why some Cárdenas residents still look suspiciously at any drink that's too sweet.

So the next time you're in Cuba and someone offers you an unknown drink, remember the legend of Son 14. And if after drinking it you hear someone say "Wait for me on the ground," well, you know what's coming. Accept your fate with dignity, or at least with what little dignity you have left after a few drinks.

Cheers, friends! And may your parties always be memorable... but for the right reasons. May the spirit of Son 14 (but not its content) always be with you, reminding you that in life, as in drinking, sometimes it's better to stick with the classics.

And remember: drinking in moderation isn't just advice, it's a survival strategy. Because, as the old Cuban philosophers said: "The happiest person isn't the one who drinks the most, but the one who remembers where they left their pants at the end of the night."

Until the next alcoholic adventure, my dear readers! And may God have mercy on your livers and your dignity.

Chapter IV: Mambí Cocktails: When Aguardiente Became Patriotic.

My friends, settle into your chairs (or hammocks, or whatever you have at hand) and prepare for a journey to the past, to an era where aguardiente wasn't just a drink, but an act of rebellion. Welcome to the era of mambí cocktails, where every drink was a declaration of independence and every hangover, a small price to pay for freedom.

The Alcoholic Counterpoint: Céspedes vs. Spanish Wine.

Imagine the scene: July 4, 1868, celebration of the independence of the Thirteen Colonies. All progressive Cubans raising glasses of wine... except Don Carlos Manuel de Céspedes. Our hero, with a bottle of aguardiente in hand and probably already a bit tipsy, delivered these verses that would go down in history:

"For a Cuban it is a disgrace,

And lack of intelligence,

To toast to independence,

With sherry wine."

Basically, Céspedes said: "Toasting with Spanish wine is like celebrating your divorce while wearing your wedding ring."

Take that! A direct blow to the liver of Spanish colonialism.

The Birth of a Tradition: Patriotism with 40 Degrees of Alcohol.

After this epic poetic-alcoholic moment, drinking aguardiente became the 19th-century equivalent of sharing anti-colonialist memes on Facebook. It was rebellious, it was cool, and it burned your throat like Spanish taxes.

Soon, drinking aguardiente became as patriotic as singing the national anthem or insulting the Captain General of the day. The Spanish, for their part, didn't understand how Cubans could drink something that, in their words, "seemed more suitable for cleaning horseshoes than for human consumption." Little did they know they were fueling the fire of revolution, one drink at a time.

Taming the Monster - Cocktails by Necessity.

But of course, not everyone had Céspedes' steel-lined throat. Soon, the revolutionaries realized that if they wanted to keep the troops "hydrated" and conscious at the same time, they needed to soften things up a bit. Thus began the great mambí cocktail experimentation:

1. Aguardiente + Honey = Less chance of setting your esophagus on fire

This was the first step toward cocktail civilization. Honey not only made aguardiente more tolerable, but also provided extra calories for long nights of planning ambushes or composing décimas against Spain.

2. Aguardiente + Water = For those who wanted to "hydrate" while getting drunk

Also known as "the fool's trick." Perfect for mambíses who wanted to maintain appearances of sobriety while secretly getting as drunk as a barrel.

3. Aguardiente + Wild plants = Because if you're going to have a hangover, at least let it taste like nature

This was the mambí version of herbal medicine. Stomach ache? Add some guava. Insomnia? A touch of linden. Fear before battle? Well, that's what straight aguardiente was for.

The Manigua: Cuba's First Clandestine Bar.

The manigua (the wilderness) became the largest mixology laboratory in Cuba. It was like the Silicon Valley of cocktails, but with more mosquitoes and fewer millionaires (for now). The rules for creating a mambí cocktail were simple:

1. Base: Aguardiente (obviously). If it doesn't make you tear up when you smell it, it's not patriotic enough.

2. Sweetener: Honey, guarapo, or raw sugar. Refined sugar was for the weak and the Spanish.

3. Special touch: Any wild plant that doesn't kill you instantly. Extra points if it has medicinal or hallucinogenic properties.

4. Name: The more patriotic, the better. Bonus if it references Spain sarcastically.

Soon, the manigua was filled with improvised "bartenders," each swearing that their mixture was the one that would finally defeat the Spanish. Spoiler alert: none did directly, but they definitely helped keep morale high.

Evolution of Mambí Cocktails.

Over time, these cocktails evolved. They started as "Aguardiente or Death" and ended up as more sophisticated creations. Here are some of the hits of the era:

1. The Rusty Machete

Ingredients: Aguardiente, sour orange juice, honey, and a touch of machete rust for that authentic revolution flavor.

This cocktail was so strong it was said to be able to cut the enemy as effectively as a real machete. The additional advantage was that if you ran out of weapons, you could always throw the bottle at the enemy.

2. Weyler's Tears

Ingredients: Aguardiente, lime juice, and a pinch of salt.

Named in "honor" of the infamous Spanish general Valeriano Weyler. This cocktail was as bitter as the tears Weyler never shed for his victims. It was preferably served in a skull-shaped gourd.

3. The Sigh of Freedom

Ingredients: Aguardiente, honey, coconut water, and a breath of free air.

This was the favorite cocktail for celebrating victories. So refreshing it made you forget you were in the middle of a brutal war. For a moment, at least.

4. Independence or Death

Ingredients: Equal parts of all available aguardientes, mixed with cane juice and juice from any fruit you could find.

This was the cocktail of desperation.

When supplies were running low and morale was down, the mambíses mixed everything they had on hand. The result was a drink that made you feel invincible... until the next morning.

The True Heroes of the Mambí Bar.

While the names of Maceo, Gómez, and Martí resonated on the battlefields, other lesser-known heroes fought their own war at the improvised bars of the manigua. These are some of the cocktails that survived the war and became legends in their own right:

1. Canchánchara

The traveling cocktail par excellence. Born in the mountains of Trinidad, this concoction of aguardiente, honey, and lime conquered palates from East to West. It was said to be as good for the spirit as for curing colds. A kind of liquid penicillin, if you will.

2. Saoco

Because drinking from a coconut is very mainstream. The mambíses, always at the forefront, decided it was better to mix coconut water with aguardiente. The result: a cocktail that makes you feel like you're on vacation in the middle of a revolution.

3. Frucanga

The cocktail that makes you shout "To the machete!" even if there are no Spanish around.

With ginger, chili, and sour orange leaves, this brew was described by a Spanish soldier as a "barbarous spawn." The mambíses, of course, took this as a compliment and put it on the label.

The Jícara - The People's Glass.

Who needs Bohemian crystal when you have a güira? The jícara, made from the güira tree fruit, became the revolution's official glass. It was resistant, biodegradable, and, most importantly, abundantly available in the manigua.

It's said that José Martí himself collected jícaras in his spare time. Imagine the Apostle saying: "Comrades, today we make glasses. The revolution needs something to drink from." It's probably a myth, but we like to think that even the greatest heroes worried about the small details... like having a good glass for your drink after a hard day of fighting for independence.

The Cuba Libre - The True Hero of Independence.

Forget what encyclopedias and pretentious bartenders in Old Havana say. The Cuba Libre wasn't born in an elegant bar after the war, but in the trenches of the manigua. The original ingredients were simple: honey water, aguardiente, and lime. The cola came later, when the revolution became more... bubbly.

It's said that the name "Cuba Libre" arose in a moment of alcoholic optimism, when a particularly inspired mambí (and probably quite drunk) shouted: "For a Free Cuba!" before downing a drink.

The name stuck, the cocktail too, and the rest is history.

The addition of cola after the war was seen by some purists as an "American intervention" in Cuban cocktail culture. Others, more pragmatic, were grateful to finally have something to disguise the taste of the dubious quality aguardiente left over from the

Chapter V: Elegguá, Aguardiente and Tobacco: A Divine Party.

Dear readers, prepare to enter the most mind-blowing world of Cuban spirituality. If you thought the parties in Havana were crazy, wait until you learn how the Orishas have fun. Welcome to the chapter where heaven meets earth, and both decide it's time for a good drink and a cigar.

When the Saints Want to Party.

Imagine the scene: a santero kneeling, blowing tobacco smoke like an old locomotive and spraying drinks left and right as if he were at the wildest New Year's Eve party of his life. Is it a religious ceremony or the strangest after-party in Havana? The answer is: Yes!

In the world of Cuban Santería, the line between the sacred and the party is as thin as a bikini string in Varadero. Here, the gods don't just come down to Earth, they do so with every intention of having a good time. Who can blame them? After all, being a deity must be quite stressful work.

The Golden Rule: First the Dead (and the Saints).

In Cuba, opening a bottle without spilling a few drops "for the dead and the saints" is like going to the beach without sunscreen: a sacrilege that guarantees you burns, whether from the sun or from the disapproving gaze of your deceased grandmother.

This tradition is so ingrained that even the most hardened atheists sometimes find themselves spilling a little stream of their beer "just in case." Because in Cuba, it's better to be on good terms with those above and those below, especially if those below can decide to appear at your house at 3 in the morning to scold you for being stingy.

Apparently, even in the afterlife they appreciate a good drink. Which makes sense, if you think about it. What else are you going to do for all eternity but enjoy good rum? Play dominoes? Well, probably that too.

Orishas: The Gods with Refined Tastes.

If you thought choosing a wine for dinner was complicated, wait until you see the Orishas' menu. Each deity has their preferences, and believe me, you don't want to confuse them. It's like a divine menu where getting the order wrong can result in something worse than a bad tip:

- Warriors (Elegguá, Oggún, Oshosi): Aguardiente. Because nothing says "let's go to battle" like a good drink that makes you forget you're about to face an army.

- Changó: Rum and red wine. Because this Orisha knows that variety is the spice of life (and of the liver).

- Yemayá: Cane syrup and coconut water. For when you want something refreshing but with a touch of sweetness, like an afternoon at the beach but without sand in uncomfortable places.

- Oshún: Honey and cinnamon. Because even deities need something to sweeten their day from time to time.

- Obatalá: Cascarilla and cotton. Okay, this isn't a drink, but Obatalá likes zen and minimalist things. He's like the friend who orders water at a party.

Remembering all these preferences is like memorizing the cocktail menu of Havana's most exclusive bar, but with much more serious consequences if you get it wrong. Nobody wants to see an Orisha pouting because you brought them the wrong drink.

The Great Escape of the Orishas: A Story of Alcohol and Deception.

Now, let me tell you a story that makes your college party escapades look like child's play. This is the story of how the Orishas achieved the most epic escape in history, all thanks to the power of alcohol.

It turns out that when the Orishas decided it was time for a vacation on Earth (probably tired of the slow wifi in heaven), Elenini, the god of obstacles and basically the official party pooper of the Yoruba pantheon, decided he wanted to join. He was like that coworker who invites himself to all the office outings.

But Orunmila, the divine fortune-teller and apparently the brains of the group, had a plan worthy of "Ocean's Eleven":

1. Make "ebbó" (ritual cleansing) with Otí (alcoholic beverage). Because, what better way to prepare for a trip than with a good "internal cleansing" session?

2. Get Elenini drunk. Yes, the plan was basically to turn the trip preparation into the wildest bachelor party in the universe.

3. Escape while the party pooper slept it off. Because even the gods know there's nothing deeper than the sleep of someone who's overdone it with aguardiente.

The plan worked perfectly. While Elenini snored like a bear with breathing problems, the Orishas made their great escape to Earth.

Moral of the story: Even the gods know that alcohol can be the solution... and the problem. It's like that crazy night that helps you forget your problems, but creates new ones the next day.

The Three Sips Ritual: When Spitting is Good Manners.

Now, prepare for the strangest and most Cuban ritual you can imagine: the three sips ritual.

In Santería, spraying the Orisha with three sips of drink isn't bad manners or the result of having drunk too much.

It is, in fact, a way to remember how they defeated Elenini and managed to reach Earth. It's basically a divine toast, but instead of saying "Cheers!" it's more like "Take that, Elenini, you played us but here we are!"

The ritual goes like this:

1. You take a sip of the Orisha's preferred drink (consult the divine menu mentioned above).

2. You spray a little in front of the altar or representation of the Orisha.

3. You repeat two more times, because good things come in threes.

4. Finally, you drink a little yourself, because after so much spitting, you've earned it.

It's like a spitting game for adults, but with religious meaning. And yes, it's perfectly acceptable, and even expected, that you make a mess. In fact, the bigger the mess, the happier the Orishas will be. It's probably the only time in your adult life when your parents would be proud to see you spitting everywhere.

Elegguá: The Orisha Who Knows How to Party.

And now, ladies and gentlemen, let me introduce you to the star of this divine show: Elegguá, the Orisha who makes all the others seem boring in comparison.

Elegguá is the warrior, the trickster, the one who opens and closes paths, and apparently, the life of the party in the Yoruba pantheon. For this Orisha, nothing like tobacco and aguardiente. He's like that friend who always knows where the party is and has a cigar to share.

His ritual is quite a spectacle:

1. Two glasses of aguardiente on Mondays. Because even Orishas hate Mondays and need something to cheer them up at the start of the week.

2. Light a tobacco. Who said smoking was bad? When it comes to pleasing Elegguá, even the surgeon general looks the other way.

3. Say: "I share with you Elegguá, aguardiente and tobacco. Give me money and open my paths." Basically, you're asking him to be your fortune agent and your personal GPS in one phrase.

4. Spray one glass over Elegguá's stone and drink a sip from the other. Because sharing is living, even when you're sharing with a stone.

5. Smoke the tobacco, alternating between taking puffs and blowing smoke over Elegguá's stone. It's like a game of "Simon Says" but with a cigar.

This whole ritual is like a private party between you and Elegguá. He gets his aguardiente and tobacco, and you, hopefully, get him to open the paths to prosperity. It's a pretty fair deal, if you ask me.

Tobacco: The Most Divine Cigar.

Now, let's talk about tobacco. In Santería, tobacco isn't just a vice, it's practically a divine communication instrument. It's like the WhatsApp of the Orishas, but with more flavor and fewer emojis.

Tobacco smoke is considered a vehicle for carrying messages to the spiritual world. It's like sending an email, but much more dramatic and with a significantly higher risk of accidental fires.

Each Orisha has their tobacco preferences:

- Elegguá prefers strong, short cigars. Like himself: small but powerful.

- Changó goes for big, thick cigars. Because everything about Changó has to be big and flashy.

- Yemayá and Oshún prefer mild cigarettes. Because even goddesses need to maintain their elegance.

So the next time you see someone blowing smoke like a chimney in the middle of summer, don't judge. They might be in the middle of an important video conference with the Orishas.

Conclusion: Santería, The Religion with the Best After Party.

And so, dear readers, we come to the end of our journey through the world of Elegguá, aguardiente, and tobacco in Cuban Santería. As we've seen, this isn't just a religion it's the most divine party you've ever witnessed.

Aguardiente in Santería is more than a simple drink it's a bridge between the divine and the human, a social lubricant for relationships between gods and mortals.

It's living proof (or should I say, fermented) that even the most elevated beings enjoy a good drink and a cigar from time to time.

So the next time you see someone blowing smoke and spraying aguardiente everywhere, don't be scandalized. They're not having a psychotic episode or trying to put out an invisible fire. They're probably just having a friendly chat with Elegguá, asking him to open some paths and, hopefully, close the path to tomorrow's hangover.

Remember: in Santería, every drink is a prayer, every puff of smoke is a message to the beyond, and every drop spilled is an offering. It's the only religion where you can say "I'm practicing my spiritual beliefs" while you're in a bar at 3 in the morning.

Cheers, and may the saints accompany us... preferably with a good drink and a cigar!

Chapter VI: Rum Stories.

The Birth of a Winged Myth.

Imagine Santiago de Cuba, 1862. The Bacardí brothers buy a distillery and, like good 19th-century entrepreneurs, decide they need a cool mascot. A lion? Too mainstream. An eagle? Too patriotic. A bat? Bingo! Because nothing says "drink me" like a nocturnal flying mammal.

The Bat: From Stowaway to Star

The bat's story is worthy of a Hollywood script:

1. Bacardí buys used barrels of olive oil (because recycling was trendy since 1862).

2. The barrels had a bat as their logo (apparently, olive oil needed a gothic touch).

3. People start asking for "the bat rum" (because "rum" alone was too boring).

4. Bacardí says: "If you can't beat them, adopt them as your logo."

And so, my friends, a bat became the face of one of the world's most famous rums. It's as if Batman decided to open a liquor store.

For almost a century, Bacardí reigned supreme. It was the Brad Pitt of rums: handsome, famous, and everywhere. But then came 1959, and with the revolution, came the plot twist:

- The government says: "All companies are ours now."

- Bacardí says: "We're leaving, but we're taking the recipe."

- Cuba says: "Take whatever you want, but the flavor stays."

The Secret Is in the Soil (And No, We're Not Talking About Burying the Rum)

It turns out that making Bacardí rum outside of Cuba is like trying to make Neapolitan pizza on Mars. They were missing key ingredients:

- Cuban soil (apparently, it has magical properties).

- The cane fields (because Cuban cane has swing).

- The wind (which blows rum, obviously).

- The sun (which in Cuba shines with rum flavor).

- The final molasses (the best-kept secret after the Coca-Cola formula).

- Cuban barrels (which are like wine barrels, but with more rhythm).

Bacardí continues to be great, nobody denies that. But it's like those Cubans who left: they can take grandma's recipe, but it will never taste the same without the island's seasoning.

The lesson here is clear: you can take the rum out of Cuba, but you can't take Cuba out of the rum. It's like trying to make a flamingo dance salsa: simply, some things belong where they belong.

So the next time you drink a Bacardí, remember: you're drinking the nostalgia of a bat that flew too far from home. Cheers, and long live rum... wherever it's made!

Ron Matusalén: The Cuban Youth Elixir (with Dominican Passport).

In Santiago de Cuba, the Camp brothers and Evaristo Álvarez decided the world needed a rum as long-lived as the biblical Methuselah. Their mission? Create a rum so smooth that even teetotalers would say: "Well, just one more."

Inspired by brandies and cognacs (because, why not give the Caribbean a French touch?), they created a recipe so secret that not even CIA spies during the Revolution could decipher it.

Matusalén shone in Cuba's crazy years. Havana was the playground for Americans fleeing Prohibition. Imagine Las Vegas, but with more mojitos and fewer slot machines.

With Castro's arrival, Matusalén packed its bags faster than a tourist in a hurricane. The family went into exile, taking the recipe but leaving behind Cuba's flavor. It's like taking the sheet music but forgetting the instrument.

In the 90s, Dr. Claudio Álvarez decided that curing hangovers was less fun than causing them. He won control of the company in a legal battle that probably lasted longer than the rum's aging process.

Today, Matusalén is produced on Dominican soil. It turns out rum is like those grandparents who move to a warmer climate but still cook just as well.

In 2002, Matusalén resurfaced as premium rum. It was no longer the rum of the Cuban party, but the favorite of connoisseurs with refined taste and bulging wallets.

Matusalén proved that quality survives exile. It's the rum that has lived more adventures than Indiana Jones, but still maintains its flavor.

So when you taste a Matusalén, remember: you're drinking a piece of Cuban history with a Dominican accent. Cheers, and long live traveling rums!

The Arechabalas: The Basque Epic That Got Cuba Drunk (and Almost the World).

It was 1862, and while the rest of the world was busy with boring things like the American Civil War, a 15-year-old Basque young man named José Arechabala decided that Gordejuela, Vizcaya, wasn't exciting enough. So he did what any sensible teenager would do: he boarded the Hermosa Trasmiera bound for Cuba.

Because, clearly, when you think of Basques, the first thing that comes to mind is rum, beaches, and salsa.

Imagine the scene: a Basque boy arriving in Cuba, probably wondering why he traded the green mountains for a place where the air is so thick you can cut it with a machete. But hey, at least the rum was cheaper than in Bilbao.

After some years working for others (probably asking himself every day why he left the cool climate of Vizcaya for the Caribbean oven), José decided it was time to be his own boss.

In 1878, he founded the La Vizcaya still in Cárdenas. Because if you can't bring the beach to Euskadi, you bring Euskadi to the beach, right?

What began as a modest still soon became an empire that would make Caribbean pirates look like amateurs selling lemonade on the corner. Arechabala S.A. didn't just produce rum they had cane plantations (because sugar doesn't grow on trees, in case anyone doubted it), refineries (to turn that cane into liquid gold), shipyards (because how else were you going to get the rum to Florida? Swimming?) and even candy factories (because after so much rum, something sweet comes in handy). Basically, if something could be done with sugar, they did it.

But the Arechabalas weren't just magnates with straw hats and daiquiris in hand. They turned out to be surprisingly decent bosses, something like Santa Claus, but with better tan and a distillery instead of a toy workshop.

They offered scholarships (because an educated worker makes better rum), medical insurance (in case someone overdid it testing the product), and even raffled houses among their employees (imagine that company Christmas party). It was as if they had created their own welfare state, but with more rum and less paperwork.

When a hurricane hit Cárdenas in 1933, Arechabala S.A. decided it was time to play government. They rebuilt the pier (because how were ships with more barrels going to arrive?), landscaped the city (rum and nature, the perfect combination) and even erected a monument to the Cuban flag (patriotism with 40 degrees of alcohol).

They practically turned Cárdenas into the Bilbao of the Caribbean, but with more palm trees and less txakoli. It was as if they had decided that if they were going to dominate the rum industry, they might as well have their own city while they were at it.

Havana Club: The Rum That Conquered America (Legally, This Time).

The crown jewel arrived in the 30s with the birth of Havana Club. Just when the United States was repealing Prohibition, the Arechabalas said: "Hey, what if we sell them something actually worth drinking instead of that bathtub alcohol they've gotten used to?"

The Americans, tired of drinking anything that could make an engine run, embraced Havana Club as if it were water in the desert. Suddenly, drinking Cuban rum was cooler than jazz and more popular than Chicago gangsters.

To top off their alcoholic dominion, the Arechabalas opened a private Havana Club bar in Cathedral Square in Havana. Because nothing says "we respect the church" like a rum bar right next door. It was the place where high society went to "pray" their liquid prayers and where more than one American tourist found their spiritual "enlightenment" (and probably a monumental hangover).

For more than 80 years, the company weathered wars, regime changes, economic crises, and even Prohibition in the U.S. It was as if they had a lucky charm bathed in rum or as if Elegguá himself (the orisha who opens paths in Cuban Santería) was their operations director.

They survived the Wars of Independence (because even in war, people need a drink), both world wars (providing the liquid fuel necessary to celebrate peace), and more political changes than cocktails on their menu.

The Arechabalas didn't just create a rum empire, they practically adopted an entire city. They proved that with enough rum, hard work, and a bit of Basque madness, you can conquer the Caribbean without needing pirates or galleons.

Their impact was so great that you couldn't understand Cárdenas without Arechabala, nor Arechabala without Cárdenas. It was as if they had created their own version of Willy Wonka and the Chocolate Factory, but with rum instead of chocolate and happy workers instead of Oompa Loompas.

When the Cuban Revolution arrived in 1959, the Arechabalas probably thought it was just another change they would survive. After all, they had been through wars, hurricanes, and prohibitions. How bad could a group of bearded men with revolutionary ideas be?

It turned out to be quite bad for the family business. But even after the family had to go into exile, the legacy of Havana Club rum continued. It's as if the spirit of the Arechabalas (and we're not just referring to the rum) continued living in every bottle.

Conclusion: A Toast to the Basques Who Conquered Cuba.

So the next time you enjoy a Cuban rum, remember those crazy Basques who decided the Caribbean needed a touch of Euskadi. Raise your glass and toast to José Arechabala and his family, who proved that with enough determination, hard work, and rum, you can conquer a country without needing an armada.

They proved that entrepreneurial spirit can take you from the Basque mountains to Caribbean beaches, and that good rum can be the best cultural ambassador. They created more than a brand they created a legend that lives on in every bottle of Cuban rum.

The Arechabalas taught us that life, like good rum, improves with time. That sometimes you have to leave your comfort zone (like the Basque Country) to find your true passion (like making the world's best rum).

And that, in the end, it doesn't matter where you come from, but what you build and the legacy you leave.

Cheers, or as they would say in Basque, Topa! For the Arechabalas, for Cuba, and for all those who dare to pursue their dreams, even if it means crossing an ocean and trading txakoli for rum.

Chapter VII: The Arechabalas, curiosities: A Cuban Saga with More Twists Than a Well-Shaken Daiquiri.

In 1921, the company adopted the name José Arechabala S.A. Don José, at 77 years old, became the first president. Imagine the scene: an elderly Basque running a rum empire from a rocking chair, probably wondering if all this was better than staying in Vizcaya growing txakoli.

Here's where the Arechabala story takes a turn worthy of a Cuban soap opera (if Cuban soap operas about rum-producing families existed).

1923: Don José dies. Apparently, making rum isn't the recipe for immortality.

1924: A son-in-law is murdered by kidnappers. Lesson learned: being a rum magnate's son-in-law can be dangerous to your health.

1926: Another son-in-law dies young. At this point, the bachelors of Cárdenas probably thought twice before courting an Arechabala.

Then, don José's daughter becomes the target of extortionists. The police, in a move worthy of "Mission Impossible," disguise an agent as a woman to catch the criminals.

Imagine the scene: a Cuban policeman with a wig and high heels, trying to walk like a high society lady while carrying a bottle of rum as a "purse."

With so much drama, most of the heirs decided it was time for a long vacation in Europe. They received their dividends from a distance, probably toasting with French champagne while longing for Cuban rum.

Meanwhile, a young man named José Fermín Iturrioz y Llaguno, nicknamed Josechu (because apparently José wasn't Basque enough), was about to become the unexpected savior of the company.

Josechu arrived in Cuba at 12 years old. At 13, he was already the "man of the house." At 17, he started working with his godfather. And at 26, in 1926, he became the head of the entire operation. It's as if Harry Potter, instead of going to Hogwarts, had gone to a distillery school.

When Josechu took the reins, Cárdenas was in decline. The port was so shallow that big ships passed by, probably mocking as they sailed toward Matanzas or Havana.

Imagine the dialogue:

Captain: "Is that the port of Cárdenas?"

Sailor: "Yes, captain."

Captain: "Ha, ha, ha. Next stop, Havana."

The docks were so bad that even the rats considered moving to more elegant places.

 Josechu's Grand Project: Because Every King Needs His Castle (or Port)

In 1933, a cyclone hit Cárdenas. Josechu, instead of crying over spilled rum, decided it was time for a change. "A modern port? Sure! Why not?"

In 1939, port dredging began. It was like a sandcastle project, but on an industrial scale and with much more rum involved.

In the 40s, Arechabala S.A. decided that making only rum was boring. Why not make candy too? They contracted Charms, the American candy giant, to build a factory.

During World War II, this factory employed more than 1,000 workers. Apparently, in times of war, people need both alcohol and sugar. Coincidence? I don't think so.

Arechabala S.A.'s production was as varied as the steps of a Cuban salsa:

- Havana Club Rum (of course)

- Relicario Brandy (for those who wanted to feel fancy)

- Arechabala Creams (because sometimes you need something smooth)

- Quirinal Vermouth (for those who wanted to feel Italian)

- Arechabala Cognac (for those who wanted to feel French)

- Caña Rum (for the purists)

- Natural alcohol and fuels (in case your car also wanted to join the party)

And as if that weren't enough, they were also pioneers in using bagasse to make paper. Because when you make so much rum, you need something to write down all those brilliant ideas that occur to you after the third glass.

 The End of an Era: When the Revolution Said "No More Rum for You!"

In the 60s, the socialist revolution decided it was time for the state to take charge of getting people drunk. Arechabala was nationalized faster than it takes to serve a mojito in Old Havana.

Josechu Iturrioz, our Basque-Cuban hero, had to say goodbye to his rum and candy empire. He went to New York, where he probably spent his last days longing for Cuba's heat and wondering if New York rum tasted like anything more than tears and nostalgia.

Although the Arechabalas left, their rum stayed. It's as if don José's spirit (and I don't mean the rum) continued wandering the streets of Cárdenas, making sure every bottle of Havana Club was perfect.

Today, you can find Havana Club in convertible currency stores, shining like a beacon of hope for thirsty tourists. Meanwhile, in popular bodegas, the Arecha brand is consumed as if it were water. Apparently, the revolution couldn't change Cubans' taste for good rum.

Conclusion: A Toast to the Arechabalas.

The Arechabala story is like good rum: complex, with notes of tragedy, success, and an ending that leaves you wanting more. They created a product that transcended their time, survived revolutions, and continues to be the soul of many Cuban parties.

So the next time you raise a glass of Cuban rum, toast to the Arechabalas. For the Basque who came to Cuba to make rum, for the boy who became king of alcohol, for the sons-in-law who didn't survive the rum curse, and for all those who ever dreamed of creating something that would last longer than themselves.

And remember: in life, as in rum, sometimes the best things come from the most unexpected places. You might start as a Basque boy on a Caribbean island and end up creating an empire. Or you might just end up with a good drunk and a great story to tell. Either way, cheers!

Guayabita del Pinar: The Liqueur That Put Pinar del Río on the Map (And in Our Livers).

Welcome to the fascinating world of Guayabita del Pinar, that "unique and divine nectar" that still hasn't found classification in the macho and masculine universe of rum. It's like the Mulan of liqueurs: it disguises itself as rum, but has a guava heart.

If you ever find yourself in Cuba's westernmost province, Pinar del Río, you'll probably be looking for the famous Habanos. But while you're there, breathing that tobacco aroma that would make even steel lungs want to smoke, you'll encounter another local treasure: Guayabita del Pinar.

It was 1892 when Lucio Garay Zabala, the eighth son of a Spanish couple (because apparently having seven children wasn't enough excitement), decided the world needed another liqueur. Using the same techniques of winemaking art, he converted the mixture of small guava and rum that peasants drank to warm up into something more sophisticated. Because, why settle for coffee when you can start your day of field work with a fruity cocktail?

Each bottle contains two or three guavas. Yes, you read that right. It's as if each bottle were a miniature tropical party. And it comes in two versions: dry (for those who want to feel adult) and sweet (for those who still have a child's soul... with permission to drink).

Nobody dares to classify it. It's not rum, it's not whiskey, it's not... well, nobody knows exactly what it is. It's like that weird uncle at family reunions that nobody knows how he's related, but everyone wants him there. All we know is that it's "the tasty liqueur of Vueltabajo." And that's enough for us.

Like every good Cuban legend, Guayabita's origins are lost in time. Apparently, it all began when some Spanish families decided that Spain was too boring and moved to the banks of the Cuyaguateje River to grow tobacco.

Because, what better way to start the day than with a little liqueur before going to work under the Caribbean sun?

Nobody knows exactly how that chance encounter between the little guava and the old liqueur occurred. It was like the alcoholic equivalent of "Beauty and the Beast": a delicate fruit falls in love with a rough liqueur, and together they create magic. Add a little sugar, and voilà, you have a prodigy in your hands (and in your liver).

In 1892, Guayabita stopped being a homemade experiment and became an industrial production. It moved to a big house on Isabel Rubio Street, between Sol and Virtudes. Because every good liqueur needs an elegant address.

In 1925, Guayabita received the Gold Medal at the International Fair of Rome. Yes, that Cuban liqueur gave a lesson to European wines and cognacs at their own game. It's like a Cuban baseball team winning the Cricket World Series.

In 1962, "Casa Garay" became the Beverages and Liqueurs company of Pinar del Río. Because if you're going to have a revolution, better have it with a good drink in hand. Production was expanded, and Aguardiente Coronilla was added to the family. Because a revolution needs variety.

With only 34 workers, the factory reached annual productions of 720,000 bottles. It's as if each worker were a little genie in a lamp, but instead of granting wishes, they produced liqueur.

In 1977, a rescue effort in production began due to great demand. Apparently, not even communism could stop Cubans' love for their Guayabita. New equipment and laboratory means were acquired to maximize quality. Because if you're going to drink, better make it something good, right?

Today, Guayabita del Pinar continues to be one of Cuba's most delicious drinks, with more than a century of antiquity and permanence. It's like the cool grandfather we'd all like to have: old, wise, and always ready for the party.

It's not easy to get, but it's recommended that at least once in your life you have the opportunity to taste this marvel from the world of liqueurs. It's like the Everest of Cuban beverages: difficult to reach, but the view (or in this case, the flavor) from the top is worth it.

Guayabita del Pinar is more than a liqueur. It's liquid history, bottled tradition, and a party in every sip. It's the pride of Pinar del Río and Cuba's best-kept secret (well, after whatever they put in their cigars).

So the next time you're in Cuba, put aside the mojito for a moment and look for a bottle of Guayabita. It might be hard to find, but hey, the best things in life are never easy. And who knows, after a couple of drinks, you might feel like you've discovered the secret of life... or at least the secret of how to have a truly Cuban hangover.

And remember, as they say in Pinar del Río: "Life is short, art is long, and Guayabita... well, that runs out too fast." Cheers!

Chapter VIII: Master Rum Makers: The Modern Druids Who Transform Water into Liquid Gold.

Introduction: When Asterix Moved to the Caribbean.

Imagine for a moment that Asterix and his friends, instead of falling into a cauldron of magic potion when they were small, had fallen into a barrel of Cuban rum. Welcome to the fascinating world of Master Rum Makers, the modern druids who, instead of resisting the Romans, resist the temptation to drink their own creation (at least during working hours).

The Druids: More Than Long Beards and White Tunics.

Before diving into the world of rum, let's take a little trip to the past. The druids, those mysterious characters we all associate with Asterix or the stones of Stonehenge (because apparently they liked playing Jenga on a monumental scale), were the wise men of ancient Celtic culture.

These bearded gentlemen were a kind of human Swiss Army knife: judges, teachers, healers, and fortune-tellers.

They were like Google, but with a tunic and no need for WiFi.

And best of all: they were experts in secret potions. Sounds familiar, doesn't it?

Speaking of potions, we can't forget Panoramix, the star druid of Asterix. This gentleman was basically the Steve Jobs of magic potions: the only one capable of creating that drink that gave superhuman strength to the Gauls.

Panoramix was tall, thin, with a white beard that would make Santa Claus envious, and always carried a golden sickle. Because, you know, cutting mistletoe with a normal sickle is too mainstream.

His magic potion was the Celtic equivalent of Red Bull: it gave you wings... to hit Romans. And like our Master Rum Makers, Panoramix jealously guarded his recipe. It was the "from druid mouth to druid ear" of antiquity.

Master Rum Makers: Panoramix with Guayabera.

Now, let's jump to the present and meet the true heroes of our story: Cuban Master Rum Makers. These modern magicians are the Panoramix of the Caribbean, but instead of giving superhuman strength, they give you the superhuman ability to dance salsa until dawn.

Like the druids, Master Rum Makers transmit their knowledge orally. It's like a game of broken telephone, but with much more delicious consequences.

The Caribbean Magic Potion: Cuban Rum.

Cuban rum has no secrets in its manufacture... or so they say with a wink. According to our Caribbean druids, the quality of their elixir isn't due to a formula kept in a safe (although they surely have one to store special bottles), but to "a culture inherited and transmitted from generation to generation, from Cuban to Cuban, from heart to heart." It's like grandma's recipe, but with much more alcohol.

Apparently, Cuba has the gift of sugarcane. It's as if the island were a giant magnet for this plant. Sugarcane grows there so admirably that even palm trees feel envious.

The molasses extracted from this magic cane has a natural microflora that makes Cuban aguardiente something truly special. It's as if each drop of rum had its own microscopic party ecosystem.

The process of making rum is like raising a child: it requires love, patience, and occasionally makes you want to drink. From sugarcane cultivation to final distillation, every step is crucial. It's like a cooking recipe, but if you mess up, instead of a ruined dinner, you have thousands of liters of wasted alcohol. No pressure.

Master Rum Makers: Druids with Taste Sense

Master Rum Makers are like superheroes, but instead of capes, they wear guayaberas. Their superpowers include:

1. Identifying and selecting raw materials (they can smell bad sugarcane from kilometers away).

2. Designing equipment and introducing technological improvements (they're like the MacGyvers of rum).

3. Maintaining the historical quality of national rums without essences or artifices (because Cuban rum is like a diva: natural and without retouching).

These rum magicians can identify each stage of the elaboration process until reaching the final blend. It's as if they had taste buds with built-in GPS.

The final blend of rum is made with all the creativity born from Cuban identity, culture, and mestizaje. It's as if each bottle were a small liquid work of art, a Picasso you can drink.

In Cuba, they're not simply called Master Rum Makers. Oh, no. They're "Masters of Cuban Rum." It's like being a knight of the Round Table, but with more rum and less uncomfortable armor.

This category implies a permanent and direct identification with the country's rum heritage and culture. It's like having a doctorate in History, Chemistry, and Party, all in one.

The Caribbean Druid Magicians: Friends of Dionysus (and All of Us)

Master Rum Makers are the true druid magicians of Cuba. They're like friends of Dionysus (the Greek god of wine and party), but with a tropical touch.

Every day, these Caribbean druids prepare their secret potions that make us feel proud of Cuban rum. It's as if each bottle were a small liquid flag of Cuba.

Cuba: The Mecca of Rum (And Epic Parties)

Cuba is to rum what France is to wine, what Germany is to beer, what Russia is to vodka. It's the promised land of rum, the place where this golden elixir flows as if it were water.

From Cuban rum were born famous cocktails like the Cuba Libre (which has little free after the third glass), the Mojito (the perfect drink for pretending you're healthy while drinking alcohol), and the Daiquiri (Hemingway's favorite smoothie).

So the next time you raise a glass of Cuban rum, remember that you're not just drinking alcohol. You're drinking history, culture, and the magic of generations of Master Rum Makers.

You're tasting the result of years of experience, of secrets whispered from master to apprentice, of full moon nights mixing magic potions (or at least that's how I like to imagine it).

You're savoring the work of modern druids, those magicians who transform sugarcane into liquid gold. Those Panoramix of the Caribbean who, instead of resisting the Romans, help us resist sobriety.

So raise your glass, close your eyes, and for a moment, imagine you're in that Gallic village, surrounded by irreducible Cubans, toasting life with the Caribbean's magic potion.

And remember: like Asterix's potion, Cuban rum also gives you superpowers. It makes you dance like a professional, sing like an angel (at least that's what you think), and speak several languages (although nobody else understands them).

Cheers, and long live the rum druids!

Chapter IX: Hemingway's Daiquiri: A Havana Odyssey.

In a twist of fate that not even Ernest Hemingway himself could have imagined in his most delirious tales, a group of American and Cuban bartenders found themselves sweating as if they were mixing cocktails in the boilers of hell. The setting for this peculiar meeting was none other than Colón Cemetery in Havana, a place where the dead rest and, apparently, the living decide to throw impromptu parties.

The Cuban sun, relentless as a literary critic facing a writer's first novel, punished our protagonists mercilessly. There they were, a handful of modern alchemists, masters of the shaker and cocktail craft, gathered in front of the tomb of Constantino "Constante" Ribalaigua. For those uninitiated in the world of Havana mixology, Constante was the equivalent of Leonardo da Vinci, but instead of painting the Mona Lisa, he had perfected the art of the daiquiri.

Chapter 2: The Legendary Constante.

Constante, a Catalan with more flair than a well-prepared margarita, had been for 35 years the undisputed king of Floridita, that temple of Havana cocktail culture where dreams were served in cocktail glasses and hangovers were as epic as Hemingway's novels.

Our hero barman had achieved the feat of converting a simple mixture of rum, lime, and ice into the coolest drink in Old Havana. It was as if he had discovered the Coca-Cola formula, but with a significantly higher alcohol percentage and a flavor that made even the most hardened teetotalers consider joining the party.

Chapter 3: The Daiquiri Ceremony.

With a silence as thick as a poorly made mojito, the tribute began in front of Constante's mausoleum. Christian Delpech, an Argentine-American barman with more accent than a tango sung by Julio Iglesias, exclaimed with tears in his eyes (or maybe it was just sweat running down his forehead):

"This is like meeting the Beethoven of cocktail making! It's bigger than discovering that mojitos have mint!"

And so, between drops of sweat that could well have been used to give a salty touch to some exotic cocktail, the bartenders began preparing rounds of daiquiri. The tinkling of the shakers sounded like a metallic symphony, an alcoholic requiem for the fallen master.

Chapter 4: Hemingway and the Diabolic Daiquiri.

You can't talk about Constante without mentioning his most famous client and, probably, the one who gave him the most work: Ernest Hemingway.

Good old "Papa," as he liked to be called (although he would doubtfully have been an example of a father figure), had a special recipe: daiquiri with double rum, grapefruit juice, and no sugar.

Basically, a cocktail that could knock out an elephant but for Hemingway was barely an appetizer.

Constante not only prepared these lethal brews for Hemingway, but was also his drinking companion. One wonders how Hemingway managed to write anything coherent after a few rounds of these "diabolic daiquiris." Perhaps therein lay the secret of his concise style: when you see double, you tend to write half.

Chapter 5: The Statue That Drinks.

In Floridita, as a perpetual reminder of their most illustrious client (and possibly the one who left the most money in the till), there's a life-size bronze statue of Hemingway. It's leaning on the bar, as if eternally waiting for its next daiquiri. Tourists take photos with it, probably thinking: "Look, honey, I've had a drink with Hemingway!"

Legend has it that on full moon nights, when the last customer has left and only the barman remains cleaning glasses, the statue comes to life and asks for one last drink. Of course, this is as true as Hemingway being a teetotaler, but who doesn't like a good story after a couple of daiquiris?

Chapter 6: The Eternal Toast.

The tribute to Constante marked the beginning of celebrations for Floridita's bicentennial. Two hundred years of history, of daiquiris served, of inspired (or dizzy) writers, of loves found and lost in the alcoholic haze of a Havana night.

Ricky Gómez, a bartender from New Orleans with more Cuban blood in his veins than rum in a Cuba Libre, declared emotionally:

"I'm happier than a kid in a candy factory. This is like winning the cocktail lottery!"

And so, under Cuba's relentless sun, this group of modern alcohol alchemists toasted to Constante, to Hemingway, to the daiquiri, and to Cuba. They raised their glasses to the sky, as if they wanted the very gods of cocktail making to join the celebration.

Epilogue: The Liquid Legacy.

At the end of the day, when the cemetery returned to its usual silence and the bartenders went back to their respective bars in Havana and the United States, there was a feeling in the air that something magical had happened. Maybe it was the alcohol, maybe the heat, or maybe the spirit of Constante and Hemingway that, without doubt, had been present in spirit (and in spirits).

What's certain is that Floridita, Constante, and the daiquiri are more than simple names in cocktail history. They're symbols of an era, of a lifestyle, of a way of understanding the world through the crystal of a cocktail glass.

So the next time you're in Havana and find yourself at Floridita's bar, order a daiquiri. And when you do, remember to raise your glass in a silent toast to Constante, to Hemingway, and to all those who have made life a cocktail worthy of being savored to the last drop.

And if you see Hemingway's statue wink at you, don't worry. It's probably the rum taking effect... or maybe, just maybe, it's old "Papa" inviting you to one last round in the great beyond. After all, what is eternity without a good daiquiri?

Chapter X: Floridita Chronicles: Where Daiquiris Flow and Legends Are Born.

Chapter 1: An Oasis in the Desert of Thirst.

Imagine, dear readers, a place where time is measured in daiquiris and stories flow as freely as rum. Welcome to Floridita, the bar that has been quenching Havana's thirst since 1817. Yes, you read that right, this temple of cocktail culture is older than most countries and definitely has better taste.

Floridita isn't just a bar it's an institution, a liquid monument to the resistance of human spirit (and spirits) against sobriety. Its slogan, "The cradle of the daiquiri," isn't just an advertising phrase it's a statement of principles, a philosophy of life distilled in a chilled glass.

Chapter 2: From Bodega to Legend.

But how did this alcoholic epic begin? Like every good story, with thirsty horses and ingenious coachmen. More than two centuries ago, in the same place where the glorious Floridita stands today, there existed a humble bodega. Its main clientele were the coachmen, who bought flour to feed their horses. Imagine the scene: horses drinking water, coachmen drinking something stronger, and the owners making money. It was the perfect virtuous circle of pre-cocktail economy.

Over time, this modest establishment evolved into "La Piña de Plata." Why a pineapple?

Well, in those times, a pineapple was more exotic than an iPhone 14 today. Besides, can you imagine a bar called "El Banano de Plata"? It doesn't have the same glamour, right?

Chapter 3: The Alcoholic Metamorphosis.

At the end of the 19th century, "La Piña de Plata" began experimenting with drink mixtures. It was like the Big Bang of Havana cocktail culture. Rum, gin, vermouth, and cognac mixed in proportions that today would make any respectable mixologist tremble. But hey, Rome wasn't built in a day, and the perfect daiquiri wasn't invented on the first shake.

In 1898, with the U.S. military intervention, the bar changed its name to "La Florida." Why? Well, imagine a thirsty marine trying to pronounce "Piña" after a few drinks. "La Florida" was easier to say and, coincidentally, reminded Americans of their last connection point with civilization before arriving in Cuba.

Chapter 4: The Birth of a Liquid Legend.

But the real magic began when Constantino Ribalaigua Vert, affectionately known as "Constante" (because "Constantino" is too long to pronounce when you're ordering your fifth daiquiri), took the reins of the bar. Constante wasn't just a barman he was an alcohol alchemist, a mixing magician, the Merlin of martinis.

Constante, along with barman Boadas Perera and chef Jan Lapont (a trio that sounds more like a law firm than a bar team), acquired the business in 1918. It was the beginning of Floridita's golden age.

Constante took the cocktail menu to the stratospheric heights of 400 proposals. More than half included lime juice, which explains why Constante had his own lime grove. Imagine: a man so dedicated to his craft that he grew his own limes. It's as if Picasso had raised his own chickens to make egg tempera paint.

Chapter 5: Hemingway, the Star Client.

And then he arrived. Ernest Hemingway, the literary giant with an equally gigantic thirst. Hemingway didn't just drink at Floridita he practically lived there. For 20 years, he occupied the same bar stool. Today, that stool is separated by a chain, as if it were the sacred relic of some patron saint of drinkers.

Hemingway didn't settle for just any daiquiri. Oh, no. He had his own version: the "Papa Doble" or "Papa Hemingway." Double rum, no sugar, with grapefruit juice. A cocktail that could knock out a bear, but for Hemingway was barely an appetizer.

Hemingway's phrase, "My mojito at La Bodeguita, my daiquiri at Floridita," became the mantra of every self-respecting tourist. It's like the "Veni, vidi, vici" of literary drinkers.

Chapter 6: Records, Recognition, and Replicas.

Floridita didn't settle for just being famous. In 1953, "Esquire" magazine rated it as one of the seven best bars in the world. It was in the same league as the Ritz in Paris and Raffles in Singapore. Not bad for a bar that started serving water to horses, eh?

But the real madness came in 2012, when they decided to prepare the world's largest daiquiri. 275 liters. 88 bottles of rum. 30 bartenders working as if their lives depended on it. It was like building the pyramids, but with more fun and fewer mummies.

Floridita has been replicated in London, Madrid, and California. It's as if the spirit of Constante and Hemingway had spread throughout the world, bringing the good news of the daiquiri to thirsty masses.

Chapter 7: Celebrities, Competitions, and Curiosities.

More celebrities have passed through Floridita than through the Oscar red carpet. Giorgio Armani, Rocky Marciano, Jean-Paul Sartre... Even the Duke and Duchess of Windsor. Imagine the scene: a boxer, an existentialist philosopher, and a duke, all sharing the bar. Sounds like the beginning of a joke, right?

Since 2015, Floridita has held an international competition to choose the "King of the Daiquiri." Participants have five minutes to prepare five glasses. It's like the Olympics, but with more alcohol and less tight clothing.

Chapter 8: The Liquid Legacy.

Today, Floridita still stands, as glorious as ever. Its 10-meter mahogany bar, its Corinthian friezes, its British Regency-style decoration... Everything remains as a testament to bygone eras, when men were men, writers were legends, and daiquiris were works of art.

The bronze statue of Hemingway, work of Villa Soberón, continues leaning on the bar, as an eternal reminder that great stories and great drinks go hand in hand. And if you ever see the statue wink at you, don't worry. It's probably the effect of the fifth daiquiri.

Epilogue: The Indomitable Spirit of Floridita.

Floridita is more than a bar. It's a monument to the resistance of human spirit (and bottled spirits). It has survived wars, revolutions, prohibitions, and, most impressively of all, Hemingway's hangovers.

So the next time you're in Havana, make a stop at Floridita. Order a daiquiri, sit at the bar next to Hemingway's statue, and raise your glass in a silent toast. Toast to Constante, to Papa, to the thirsty coachmen and their even thirstier horses. Toast to all those who have made Floridita not just a bar, but a legend.

And remember: at Floridita, as in life, what's important isn't the destination, but the journey. Although if the journey includes a few daiquiris, much better.

Chapter XI: The Art of Drinking Cuban Rum: A Guide for Aspiring Experts.

Chapter 1: Introduction to the Caribbean Elixir.

Welcome, dear apprentices of the Cuban rum school. If you're reading this, it's because you've decided to elevate your status from simple drinkers to authentic connoisseurs. Or maybe you just want to impress your friends at the next party. In either case, you're in the right place.

Cuban rum, that golden nectar that has inspired revolutions, novels, and probably some bad decisions at 3 in the morning, isn't just a drink. It's a lifestyle, a philosophy, and possibly the reason why the Cuban population always seems to be in such good humor.

Chapter 2: The Unwritten Rules (until now).

Rule 1: The Little Bit for the Saints.

Before you start thinking this is just a matter of opening a bottle and tilting it back, let me stop you right there. In Cuba, drinking rum is an almost religious ritual. And like every good ritual, it begins with an offering.

As soon as you open the bottle, head to a corner of the house and pour a small portion on the floor. No, it's not because the floor is thirsty. It's an offering to the Afro-Cuban deities. Think of it as a divine bribe to obtain abundance, health, and hopefully, avoid tomorrow's hangover.

Rule 2: The "Strike" or How to Prove You're a Macho (or Macha).

A self-respecting Cuban must, at least once, drink rum "strike style." This means: no mixers, no ice, nothing that can soften the blow. It's like an initiation rite. If you manage it without your eyes popping out of their sockets, congratulations, you can now consider yourself an honorary Cuban rum drinker.

Rule 3: The Democracy of the Glass.

Forget crystal glasses and designer cups. In Cuba, rum doesn't discriminate by container. A plastic cup, a cut can, even a shoe (although we don't recommend it for obvious hygienic reasons) will do. What's important is the content, not the container. Besides, this way there's less chance of breaking grandma's fine china when the party gets out of control.

Rule 4: The Last Drink or "The Brave One's Test".

The last drink from the bottle is sacred. It must be taken in one gulp and, if you're brave (or foolish) enough, directly from the bottle's mouth. It's like the last dance at a party, but with more chances of ending up hugging the toilet.

Rule 5: Sharing is Living.

In Cuba, good rum is the kind you share. You could have the most expensive bottle in the world, but if you drink it alone, you're simply an alcoholic with good taste. Share with friends, family, or that stranger on the street who seems to need a drink. Remember: rum is a social catalyst, not a solitary hobby.

Chapter 3: For Aspiring Rum Sommeliers.

If you want to go further and become a true connoisseur, here are some additional tips:

1. Feel the Heat: Rum is served at room temperature. Hold the glass with your hand and let your body heat warm it. It's like giving your drink a hug.

2. Choose the Right Glass: A cognac glass, an Old Fashioned glass, or a Havana Club glass are ideal. Avoid tall, narrow glasses rum needs space to breathe, like your uncle after Christmas dinner.

3. Ice in Moderation: If you're going to use ice, let it be one or two cubes maximum. Crushed ice is for cocktails and children. You're an adult now.

4. Smell Gently: Don't inhale as if it were your last breath. Bring your nose close gently, one nostril at a time. It's rum, not a drug test.

5. Savor Slowly: Let the rum dance on your tongue. Enjoy each note, each nuance. It's not a competition to see who drinks it fastest (unless it is, in which case, ignore this advice).

6. Proper Storage: Store the open bottle in a warm, dry place. The refrigerator is for beer and pizza leftovers, not for rum.

Epilogue: The True Spirit of Cuban Rum.

At the end of the day, remember that Cuban rum is more than a simple drink. It's bottled history, liquid culture, and probably the reason why Cubans dance so well.

So the next time you hold a glass of Cuban rum, remember these rules, raise your glass (whatever it may be), and toast to life, love, and the possibility that tomorrow your head won't hurt so much.

And remember, as they say in Cuba: "For every ill, rum. For every good, also. And if there's no remedy, a liter and a half."

Cheers!

Chapter XII: Cuban Rum Chronicles: A Spirited Journey Through the Sugar Island.

Prologue: Confessions of an Amateur Rum Lover.

Dear reader, if you've opened this book, it's because you share a passion with me. No, I'm not talking about collecting rare stamps or doing origami (although who knows, maybe you like those things too). I'm talking about something much nobler, more Cuban, more... alcoholic. I'm talking, of course, about rum.

Before you start thinking I'm some kind of expert in the field, let me clarify something: I'm as much an expert on rum as Hemingway was on sobriety.

That is, not much. But what I lack in technical knowledge, I make up for in enthusiasm and hours of "field research" (read: drinking rum in various situations and locations).

This book is my humble attempt to share with you, dear rum enthusiast (or nosy curious person, who are also welcome), my experiences, opinions, and ramblings about Cuba's golden nectar. If you're looking for a scientific treatise on distillation, you've made the wrong purchase. But if you want a fun journey through the world of Cuban rum, accompanied by possibly exaggerated anecdotes and advice of dubious utility, you've come to the right place!

So fasten your seatbelt (or better yet, loosen it, because we're going to drink), and join me on this spirited journey through the sugar island. Cheers!

Chapter 1: Cuba in a Bottle.

If I had to summarize Cuba in one sentence, it would be like trying to fit the Malecón into a bottle of rum: simply impossible and probably illegal. My Caribbean island is a cocktail of contradictions and wonders, shaken by history and served with a smile and a son rhythm.

But if you pressed me (and believe me, many people have, usually after the fifth round of mojitos), I'd say that rum is the distilled essence of Cuba. It's our history, our culture, our spirit (in more ways than one) bottled.

In Cuba, making rum isn't just a business it's an art, a science, and, for some, a religion. Master rum makers are like high priests of an alcoholic cult, revered for their ability to transform sugarcane into liquid gold. If there were a Vatican of rum, it would be in Havana, and the Pope would have an impressive mustache and smell slightly of molasses.

Chapter 2: The Chosen Ones (My Favorite Rums).

Now, let me share with you my personal list of the best Cuban rums under 50 dollars. Yes, I know what you're thinking: "Why 50 dollars?" Well, because even rum book writers have to pay rent. Besides, if you can afford rums over 50 dollars, you probably don't need my advice.

1. Santísima Trinidad 15 years

We start strong, as it should be. The Santísima Trinidad 15 years is the rum equivalent of that great-aunt we all have: aged, complex, and with a character that leaves you breathless.

This rum is made in three aging stages, as if it were a three-act play, but much more fun and with a happier ending.

The result is a dark amber rum, so bright you could use it as an emergency mirror if you ever need to check for food between your teeth while lost in a Cuban distillery (it's happened to me, don't ask).

Its aroma is a symphony of wood, toasted caramel, and dried fruits. It's as if someone had made a perfume with the essence of a gourmet carpentry shop. As for the flavor, it's so unctuous you could use it as a butter substitute on your morning toast (although I don't recommend it, at least not before 11 AM).

2. Havana Club Selección de Maestros.

The Havana Club Selección de Maestros is like that friend who always knows what to say at the right moment: elegant, sophisticated, and with a touch of mischief.

This rum goes through a double barrel process that's like a luxury vacation for alcohol: first it relaxes in white oak barrels and then moves to younger barrels for a touch of freshness. It's as if the rum went to a spa and then to a nightclub, all on the same day.

With 45% alcohol, this rum isn't for the weak of heart (or liver). But believe me, every drop is worth it. It's perfect for gifting, especially if the recipient is yourself.

3. Ron Edmundo Dantés Reserva 15 years.

Ah, the Edmundo Dantés. So exclusive that making a bottle of this rum is harder than finding a penguin in Havana. Only 3,000 bottles of this liquid jewel are produced, making it the rum equivalent of a winning lottery ticket.

Tasting this rum is like reading Dumas' "The Count of Monte Cristo," but instead of revenge, you find a light, smooth vanilla flavor. It's a sensory adventure that transports you to Cuba's eastern mountains, solving mysteries you didn't even know existed.

4. Cubay Añejo Suave.

The Cubay Añejo Suave is the rum drinker's best friend: reliable, affordable, and always ready for a good time. It's the rum I chase from right to left every time I set foot in Cuba, like a dog chasing its tail, but with a much nobler purpose.

Its amber color and smooth flavor with a touch of spices make it the perfect companion for any occasion, from a beach party to a García Márquez reading session by candlelight (because the power went out, not for romance).

5. Ron Cubay Reserva 10 Años.

The Ron Cubay Reserva 10 Años is like that friend who always arrives late to parties, but when he does, everyone's glad to see him. With its dark color and intense flavor of wood, dark chocolate, and pepper, it's the kind of rum that makes you question why you ever drank anything else.

Every sip of this rum is a promise that life can be better, especially if you have another bottle stored in the pantry.

6. Havana Club Añejo 7 Años.

The Havana Club 7 Años is the world's best-selling super Premium rum, making it the Messi of rums. Created by Don José Navarro, the First Master of Cuban Rum (a title that sounds like a "Game of Thrones" character, but with fewer dragons and more alcohol), this rum is living proof that patience is a virtue, especially when it comes to alcoholic beverages.

It takes more than 14 years to create Havana 7, which means this rum has spent more time maturing than most teenagers. Its "Continuous Aging" process is so complex you'd need a PhD in Quantum Physics to fully understand it. But don't worry, you don't need to understand it to enjoy it.

7. Santiago de Cuba 11 años.

The Santiago de Cuba 11 años is the rum equivalent of that friend who always has an interesting story to tell. When you smell it, experts recognize aromas of fruits and spices typically Cuban.

I, personally, only recognize that it smells incredibly good.

Produced in the province of Santiago de Cuba, this rum captures the festive essence of Cubans. Every sip is like a mini carnival in your mouth, without the need for costumes or floats.

8. Caribbean Club Reserva 7 años

Don't confuse Caribbean Club with Havana Club. It's like confusing the Weasley twins: they look the same, but each has their own personality.

This rum offers what experts call a "harmonious complexity," which is an elegant way of saying it tastes damn good. It's ideal for relaxing, which in Cuba means practically any time of day.

9. Guayabita del Pinar

The Guayabita del Pinar is the odd duck of this list, in the best possible sense. It comes in two versions: dry and sweet. The dry version is like a challenge in a bottle, while the sweet one is so smooth you could drink it for breakfast (although, again, I don't recommend it, at least not every day).

The most curious thing about this rum is the little guava floating at the bottom of the bottle. It's like finding a worm in a bottle of mezcal, but much more appetizing.

10. Ron Legendario, Elixir de Cuba 7 años.

The Ron Legendario is... well, legendary. It's so smooth and delicate that drinking it is like being caressed by a Caribbean breeze, if that breeze had 34% alcohol.

Its artisanal elaboration, which includes the use of macerated raisins, gives it a unique flavor that conquers the most demanding palate. It's the kind of rum that makes you feel sophisticated, even if you're drinking it in pajamas while watching soap operas.

Epilogue: Rum, Life, and Everything Else.

And so we come to the end of our spirited journey. I hope this tour through the world of Cuban rum has left you wanting more (rum, not more of my ramblings, although I'd appreciate both).

Remember, Cuban rum isn't just a drink it's a way of life. It's history, culture, and tradition distilled in a bottle. It's the perfect companion for celebrating good times and making bad times more bearable.

So the next time you have a bottle of Cuban rum in your hands, take a moment to appreciate it. Smell it, taste it, and if you feel especially poetic, you might even talk to it (although I recommend waiting until after the third drink to do this, for the sake of your dignity).

And if you ever find yourself in Cuba, desperately searching for me to thank me for this wonderful book, you'll probably find me in some bar in Havana, "researching" for my next bestseller. Don't hesitate to buy me a drink.After all, sharing is living, especially when it comes to good rum.

Cheers, and until the next rum adventure!

Chapter XIII: Confessions of a Rum Alchemist: Guide for Aspiring Rum Druids.

Dear intrepid reader (and possibly thirsty),

If you've made it this far, it's because we share a dangerous passion. No, I'm not talking about collecting rare stamps or skydiving in slippers (although the latter sounds quite interesting). I'm talking about something much nobler, more Cuban, and definitely more alcoholic: rum alchemy.

Before you start thinking I'm some kind of genius distiller or a master rum maker with decades of experience, let me clarify something: I'm as much an expert at mixing rums as a fish is at mountain climbing.

That is, not much. But what I lack in technical knowledge, I make up for in enthusiasm, creativity, and a total lack of common sense when it comes to experimenting with spirituous beverages.

This book, or rather, this manifesto of rum madness, is my humble attempt to share with you, dear rum enthusiast (or suicidal curious person, who are also welcome), my adventures in the world of homemade rum blends. If you're looking for a scientific treatise on distillation, you've made the wrong purchase. But if you want a fun journey through the world of "what would happen if I mix this with that?" accompanied by possibly exaggerated anecdotes and advice of dubious utility, you've come to the right place!

So fasten your seatbelt (or better yet, loosen it, because we're going to drink), put on your wizard hat (or lab coat, or both), and join me on this journey toward alcoholic madness. Cheers!

Chapter 1: The Perfect Rum Alchemist's Kit.

Before diving into the wonderful world of rum blends, you need to prepare yourself properly. Here's a list of essential elements for any aspiring rum druid worth their salt:

1. Rums (obviously): Identify your preferred and cheapest rums. Yes, I said cheapest. We don't want you to end up mortgaging your house for this noble experiment. Besides, if the blend goes wrong, you'll cry less over having wasted cheap rum than a collector's bottle. Take your time doing this, don't rush. Remember, Rome wasn't built in a day, and your rum palate won't be either.

2. Mad scientist/druid costume: Get a white lab coat, some chemical beakers, or, if you want to go to the extreme, a beard and long white wig. The goal is that when you look in the mirror, you can't help but laugh at yourself. If your neighbors start calling you "The Rum Madman," you'll know you've succeeded.

3. Time: Make sure you have enough time for these "rum reactions." Keep in mind that a Master Rum Maker, like a Druid, spends their entire life training, and you'll do it in just 15 minutes. It's like taking an intensive neurosurgery course by watching YouTube videos, but much more fun and with fewer chances of malpractice lawsuits.

4. Containers or bottles: They must be clean, have personality, and be made of transparent glass. Forget those plastic bottles you saved from the last party. We want to see the rum's "tears" rolling down the bottle, not the real tears you'll shed if your blend goes wrong.

5. A friend in love distress: Yes, you read that right. You need a guinea pig, I mean, a brave assistant willing to try your creations. Preferably someone going through a breakup who wants to "drown their sorrows."

6. You'll kill two birds with one stone: your friend will forget their heartache (and possibly their own name) and you'll have someone to test your blends without asking too many questions.

Chapter 2: The Initiation Ceremony.

Now that you have everything ready, it's time for the initiation ceremony. Follow these steps to the letter (or not, we're really improvising here):

1. Put on your mad scientist/druid costume.

2. Light some candles to create atmosphere (and to have a light source when the electricity inevitably goes out from overloading your homemade still).

3. Put on some Cuban music in the background. I recommend Buena Vista Social Club, but if you prefer reggaeton, I won't judge you (well, maybe a little).

4. Stand in front of the mirror and repeat three times: "By the power of aged rum, I invoke you, spirit of Bacardi." If nothing happens, don't worry, it's normal. If a man with a mustache and straw hat appears, you've drunk too much before starting.

Chapter 3: The Apprentice Druid's Blends.

Now, the moment we've all been waiting for.

My patented blends (not really, but it sounds good) of homemade rum.

Remember, these blends have been extensively tested by me and my team of professional tasters (read: my friends after a party night). Proceed at your own risk.

1. The Elixir of Oblivion.

Ingredients:

- 1 part Elixir Cubay 33

- 1 part Ron Legendario, Elixir de Cuba 7 years

- 1 part Cubay aged extra smooth

Instructions: Mix all ingredients in a glass bottle. Shake gently while whispering the names of your ex-partners. The result is an ultra-unique mixture of smooth flavors, perfect for starting and ending the night. It's also excellent for forgetting why you started drinking in the first place.

Variation: Substitute Ron Legendario for Guayabita del Pinar. I assure you you'll touch the sky. Or at least, you'll see the stars when you fall off your chair.

2. The Nectar of the Rum Gods.

Ingredients:

- 1 part Havana Club 7 years

- 1 part Caney aged

- 1 part Havana Club Reserve

Instructions: Combine these high-quality rums in equal proportions. The result is an exceptional rum, ready to be paired with any Habano or with a pineapple pizza (we don't judge). I put my pirate head on the line for this blend.

Advanced variation: Substitute Ron Caney for Ron Caribbean Club. You won't just touch the sky, you'll get your Rum Druid diploma without a doubt. Side effects may include the ability to talk to plants or believing you're the reincarnation of Hemingway.

3. The Forbidden Potion.

Ingredients:

- 1 part Selección de Maestros

- 1 part Santiago 11

- 1 part Cubay 10 years

Warning: This blend is only for Master Rum Makers and Druids who are direct descendants of Panoramix. If you don't know who Panoramix is, you're probably not ready for this blend.

Instructions: Combine these unique rums in a cauldron... I mean, in a glass bottle. Shake three times clockwise and once counterclockwise (this doesn't affect the flavor, but it makes you feel like a real alchemist).

Taste it alone, among incenses of anise and cinnamon. If you dare to go further, substitute the Cubay 10 years for Santísima Trinidad and you'll see with your own eyes how the Afro-Cuban deities knock on your door thirsty for adventure and divination. Or maybe it's just your neighbor complaining about the noise.

Epilogue: Rum, Life, and Everything Else.

And so we come to the end of our journey through the wonderful world of homemade rum alchemy. I hope these recipes have inspired you to explore, experiment, and, above all, not take the art of rum blending too seriously.

Remember, my friend, that rum, like life itself, should be taken with joy, in measure, and at the right moment. It's an opportunity to celebrate, to share, to forget problems, and to create new ones (like that call to your ex at 3 AM after trying "The Elixir of Oblivion").

However, like everything in life, moderation is key. Drinking without reasons and without measure leads absolutely nowhere, except maybe to a monumental headache and questionable tattoo decisions.

So, dear apprentice rum druid, I leave you with these words of wisdom:

1. Respect the rum, and the rum will respect you (or at least, it won't punish you so much the next day).

2. Share your creations with friends, but make sure they're friends who won't sue you if things go wrong.

3. Never, under any circumstances, mix rum with important responsibilities. Work meetings and rum alchemy don't get along well.

4. If at any point during your experiments you start seeing double, it's time to stop. If you start seeing triple, it's time to call a taxi.

5. And finally, always remember: in the world of rum, as in life, what's important isn't the destination, but the journey. Although if the journey includes an epic hangover, you might want to reconsider your route.

May your blends always be tasty, your hangovers mild, and may you never lack a good friend to share a glass of your latest rum creation.

Cheers, and until the next alcoholic adventure!

Translator's Note.

This translation has been completed using Claude AI with the objective of making the work of author Edo Cruz comprehensible to English-speaking readers.

The translation aimed to preserve the author's unique humor, Cuban cultural references, and colloquial writing style while adapting it naturally for an English-speaking audience.

Every effort was made to maintain the book's essence - from its irreverent tone about Cuban rum culture to its blend of historical facts and personal anecdotes.

The author's original voice, filled with wit, sarcasm, and genuine love for Cuban rum tradition, presented both challenges and opportunities in translation. Cultural references specific to Cuba, Spanish wordplay, and idiomatic expressions required careful adaptation to ensure English readers could fully appreciate the humor and cultural context.

Any errors in translation, cultural adaptation, or loss of nuance from the original Spanish text are the responsibility of Claude AI's translation process. The intent was to honor Edo Cruz's work while making it accessible to those who wish to understand and appreciate Cuban rum culture through the author's passionate and entertaining perspective.

Chapter XIV: The Art of Uncorking the Bottle: A Sacred Ritual (According to the Masters).

Dear readers, after thirteen chapters of irreverent adventures through the world of Cuban rum, it's time to get a bit more serious.

Not too serious, mind you we're still talking about alcohol here but serious enough to learn from those who really know what they're talking about.

You see, while I've been entertaining you with stories of pirates, revolutionaries, and drinks that could knock out elephants, there are actual masters of this craft who have elevated rum drinking to an art form. And one of the most important lessons they teach is something as apparently simple as opening a bottle.

The Philosophy Behind the Cork.

Now, before you roll your eyes and think "it's just opening a bottle, for crying out loud," let me stop you right there. According to the true masters of Cuban rum, the way you approach a bottle reveals everything about your relationship with the drink, with the culture, and frankly, with life itself.

As one legendary master put it: "The way we approach rum reflects our approach to life itself. Do we do it hastily and inattentively, seeking only immediate effects? Or with patience and consciousness, valuing nuances, depth, and meanings?"

Deep, right? And here I've been opening bottles like I'm defusing a bomb - quickly and hoping for the best.

The Sacred Steps (Or How to Open a Bottle Like a Zen Master).

So, after learning from the masters, here's how you should properly uncork a bottle of Cuban rum. Fair warning: this process takes longer than making a mojito, but the masters swear it's worth it.

Step 1: The Mental Preparation.

Before even touching the bottle, you need to achieve the right mental state. This means serenity, presence, and full attention. I know, I know - you just want a drink after a long day, but bear with me. The masters say rum "deserves all our attention."

Step 2: Set the Scene.

Create the right environment: temperature between 21°C and 24°C (good luck with that in Cuba during summer), sufficient lighting to appreciate colors, and no strong odors. This means put away that garlic you were chopping and maybe warn your dog that his presence might not be appreciated during this sacred ritual.

Step 3: The Initial Observation.

Hold the bottle against the light to appreciate the liquid's clarity and color. This is where you pretend to be a wine expert, except with rum, and hopefully with less pretension.

Step 4: The Recognition.

Hold the bottle with both hands for a few moments, in what the masters call "symbolic gesture of recognizing the collective work that created it." Think of all the people who made this moment possible: the cane cutters, the distillers, the barrel makers, and yes, even the guy who designed the label.

Step 5: The Uncorking.

Open the cap with precise but delicate movements. No twisting it off like you're opening a beer. This is serious business. As the masters say: "It's like opening the door to a world of sensations."

Step 6: The First Aromatic Greeting.

Bring your nose to the freshly opened bottle's mouth without agitating it. This is the rum introducing itself, saying "Hello, I'm a premium aged rum from Cuba, pleased to make your acquaintance."

Step 7: The Ceremonial Pour.

Serve the rum in an appropriate glass with fluid and controlled movement. Never fill more than one-third capacity. This isn't a beer you're not trying to get drunk quickly (well, maybe you are, but pretend you're not).

Step 8: The Visual Appreciation.

Contemplate the liquid in the glass. Look at its color, viscosity, the "tears" it forms on the crystal walls. This is where you nod knowingly and make sounds like "hmm" and "ah, yes."

Step 9: The Aromatic Approach

Bring your nose to the glass following a specific pattern: first at a distance, then progressively closer, alternating nostrils. Yes, alternating nostrils. You'll look ridiculous, but apparently, it's what the masters do.

Step 10: The First Sacred Sip.

Take a small amount and maintain it briefly in your mouth before swallowing slowly. The masters call this "recognition, not analysis." It's like shaking hands with the rum before having a proper conversation.

The Deeper Meaning (Or Why This Isn't Just Pretentious Nonsense).

Now, I'll admit, when I first heard about this ritual, I thought it was a bit much. But after trying it a few times (purely for research purposes, of course), I began to understand what the masters were getting at.

This isn't just about showing off or being pretentious. It's about connection - connection to the culture that created the rum, to the generations of knowledge that went into making it, and to the moment itself. In our rushed world, taking time to properly appreciate something is almost revolutionary.

As one master explained: "When uncorking a bottle with full consciousness, we establish connection with all who participated in its creation: from the cane cutter who cut the cane to the master who selected the barrel."

The Cuban Twist (Because We Can't Be Completely Serious).

Of course, this being Cuba, even the most sacred rituals have their practical adaptations. Here's how the average Cuban actually applies these principles:

1. Mental Preparation: "Please let this rum be good because it's all I could afford."

2. Setting the Scene: Find a place where your mother-in-law won't criticize your drinking habits.

3. Initial Observation: "Yep, it's brown. That's a good sign."

4. Recognition: "Thank you, sugarcane gods, for this gift."

5. Uncorking: Try not to break the cork because you might need to use it again.

6. First Aromatic Greeting: "Smells like... rum. Success!"

7. Ceremonial Pour: Pour into whatever clean glass you can find. Plastic cup works too.

8. Visual Appreciation: "It's not moving, so it's probably good."

9. Aromatic Approach: Smell it to make sure it won't kill you.

10. First Sacred Sip: "¡Coño! That's strong!"

Conclusion: Respect the Ritual (But Don't Lose Your Sense of Humor).

Look, the truth is that the masters are onto something. Taking time to properly appreciate good rum - or anything good in life, really - enhances the experience. It connects you to something larger than yourself and transforms a simple act into a meaningful moment.

But let's not forget that rum, at its heart, is also about joy, celebration, and sharing with friends. So yes, learn the ritual, respect the tradition, appreciate the craft - but don't forget to enjoy yourself in the process.

After all, as I've learned writing this book, the best rum experiences aren't the ones where you follow every rule perfectly. They're the ones where you share a good bottle with good people, whether you're uncorking it like a Zen master or twisting it off like you're opening a beer.

The rum doesn't care about your technique as much as it cares about your intention. Approach it with respect, appreciation, and a sense of fun, and it will reward you accordingly.

And if all else fails, just remember the most important rule of Cuban rum drinking: "Para todo mal, ron. Para todo bien, también." (For every bad thing, rum. For every good thing, also.)

¡Salud!

Author's Reflections: When Climate Goes Crazy and Sugarcane Gets Rebellious Or How to Save Cuban Rum from the Meteorological Apocalypse.

Dear companions in alcoholic adventures,

I'm taking a break between sip and sip (always responsibly, of course) to talk to you about something that keeps me awake more than Cuban coffee at 11 PM: the future of our beloved rum in these crazy times when even the climate seems to have lost its mind.

Sugarcane: From Spoiled Princess to Reality Show Survivor

Let me tell you a secret: our sugarcane has always been a bit pampered. For centuries it was Cuba's pretty girl, growing happily under our Caribbean sun like a tourist in Varadero with all-inclusive. But now, with this climate more bipolar than a teenager during exam season, poor sugarcane doesn't know if it needs an umbrella or sunscreen.

Climate change arrived in Cuba like that uncomfortable visitor who stays longer than expected and eats everything in your fridge. Hurricanes now come more frequently than power outages (and that's saying a lot), droughts last longer than a Mexican soap opera, and when it rains, it does so as if the sky had decided to unburden itself of all its problems at once.

For our sweet cane, this is like living on an emotional roller coaster without a safety belt.

Sugar Mills: From Roaring Giants to Silent Museums

The old sugar mills, those iron colossi that once made the earth tremble with their industrial roar, now many are quieter than a politician promising during election season. Some have become tourist attractions where people go to cry nostalgias while sipping a mojito.

It's like seeing your wrestler grandfather turned into an old man who feeds pigeons in the park: he retains his dignity, but he's not the same anymore.

The Domino Effect: When Everything Wobbles Like a Drunk Person on the Malecón

Here comes the worrying part: without healthy cane, there's no good sugar. Without good sugar, there's no worthy molasses. Without worthy molasses, there's no rum worth drinking. And without rum worth drinking... well, then we'd have a national crisis more serious than running out of coffee.

It's like an existential domino: if the first piece falls (the cane), the entire beautiful house of cards of rum comes tumbling down. And that, my dear readers, is unthinkable.

Cuban Solutions: Because We're Experts at Solving the Impossible

But relax, all is not lost. Cubans are like those magicians who pull rabbits out of empty hats, except we pull solutions out of problems that seemed impossible. Here are my proposals to save rum from the climate apocalypse:

1. Bionic Super Cane Why not create sugarcane more resistant than a Cuban grandfather? One that survives hurricanes, droughts, and even family political discussions. Cuban scientists are already on this, probably working with one hand while holding a little coffee with the other.

Imagine a cane that says: "Hurricane? Please! I've survived worse crises." A cane with attitude, with personality, with... well, with more resistance than patience in a bodega line.

2. Smart Irrigation: Because Even Plants Deserve Technology Implement irrigation systems that are smarter than a medical student solving a Rubik's cube.

3. Sensors that know exactly how much water each plant needs, like having a personal butler for each sugarcane stalk.

"Ms. Cane number 1,247, I see you're a bit thirsty. Allow me to serve you exactly 2.3 liters of water at perfect temperature."

3. Sweet Diversification: Because Not All Eggs Should Go in the Same Basket What if we experiment with other sugar sources? Sugar beets, tropical fruits, even coconut. We could have mango rum (imagine that!), papaya rum, rum from... well, whatever ferments and doesn't kill us in the process.

It's like having a plan B, C, D and even Z for sugar. Because diversification is the key to success, as my aunt Esperanza used to say while selling everything at her market stall.

4. Educational Tourism: Turning Problems into Opportunities Create tourist routes that show how we face climate change while producing rum. "Come and see how we save the world one bottle at a time." Tourists learn, we make money, and everyone ends up with a glass in hand. Triple win!

5. Circular Economy: Because Nothing is Wasted, Everything is Transformed Use every part of the cane as if it were ground gold. Bagasse for energy, vinasse for fertilizer, even leaves to make hats (well, maybe not so much, but the idea is to use everything).

It's like cooking with grandma: nothing gets thrown away, everything has its purpose, and in the end there's always something delicious to eat... or drink.

The Real Heroes: The People Who Make Liquid Magic

But the real hope isn't in machines or plants, but in people.

Those master rum makers who get up every day thinking "today I'm going to make something extraordinary," those workers who see cane not as a crop but as a promise of future joy.

They're like superheroes without capes, but with better stories and more experience creating liquid happiness.

The Future: Optimistic as a Cuban on New Year's Eve

Will it be easy? Please! If it were easy, anyone would make Cuban rum and then it wouldn't be special. The challenges are there, as real as the line to buy chicken, but so are the solutions, as Cuban as rice and beans.

Cuban rum has survived everything: colonizers with bad taste, revolutions, blockades, crises that would make economists cry, and now it will face climate change with the same determination with which a Cuban waits for the bus: knowing it might be late, but that it will eventually arrive.

The Final Moral (Rum Included)

At the end of the day, Cuban rum is more than fermented sugar. It's our way of telling the world: "Look, even when everything gets difficult, we keep making beautiful things."

It's bottled resistance, distilled optimism, joy that can be drunk. And as long as there are Cubans willing to get up every morning and say "let's make rum," it doesn't matter if it rains, if it's sunny, or if the climate goes crazy like a tourist without sunscreen.

Because Cuban rum, like us, always finds a way to move forward.

Call to Action (Or Responsible Toast)

So the next time you open a bottle of Cuban rum, remember: you're not just drinking alcohol, you're drinking ingenuity, resistance, and the promise that there will always be a Cuban solution to any problem.

And if after reading all this you need a drink to process the information, I understand you perfectly. Just remember to apply the Chapter XIV ritual and drink with the awareness that you're participating in a tradition that won't be defeated by a little bad weather.

Cheers to the future of Cuban rum, which will continue to be the best in the world, rain, shine, or zombie apocalypse!

P.S.: If someone invents sugarcane resistant to everything, please name it after me. "Edo Cruz Cane" sounds good, doesn't it?